STUDENT UNIT GUIDE

UNIT

3

AC

Sociology

Beliefs in Society

Joan Garrod

115253

Philip Allan Updates, an imprint of Hodder Education, an Hachette UK company, Market Place, Deddington, Oxfordshire OX15 0SE

Orders

Bookpoint Ltd, 130 Milton Park, Abingdon, Oxfordshire, OX14 4SB
tel: 01235 827720
fax: 01235 400454
e-mail: uk.orders@bookpoint.co.uk
Lines are open 9.00 a.m.–5.00 p.m., Monday to Saturday, with a 24-hour message answering service. You can also order through the Philip Allan Updates website: www.philipallan.co.uk

© Philip Allan Updates 2009

ISBN 978-0-340-97241-0

First printed 2009
Impression number 5 4 3 2 1
Year 2013 2012 2011 2010 2009

This Guide has been written specifically to support students preparing for the AQA A2 Sociology Unit 3 examination. The content has been neither approved nor endorsed by AQA and remains the sole responsibility of the authors.

Typeset by Phoenix Photosetting, Chatham, Kent
Printed by MPG Books, Bodmin

Hachette UK's policy is to use papers that are natural, renewable and recyclable products and made from wood grown in sustainable forests. The logging and manufacturing processes are expected to conform to the environmental regulations of the country of origin.

Contents

Introduction

■ ■ ■

Content Guidance

■ ■ ■

Questions and Answers

Introduction

About this guide

This unit guide is aimed at students taking the AQA A2 Sociology course. It covers the topic of **Beliefs in Society**, with a main focus on the sociology of religion, which is examined within Unit 3 (SCLY3). Beliefs in Society is one of the four choices of topic in the unit, the other three being Global Development, Mass Media and Power and Politics. The topic is designed to give you a good understanding of the importance of religion, science and ideologies to individuals and to society as a whole, as well as the different types of religious organisations and beliefs and how these have changed over time.

There are three sections to this guide:

- **This Introduction** provides advice on how to use the unit guide, an explanation of the skills required in A2 Sociology and suggestions for effective revision. It concludes with guidance on how to succeed in the unit examination.
- **The Content Guidance** section provides you with an overview of what is included in the specification for Beliefs in Society. It is designed to make you aware of what you should know before the unit examination.
- **The Questions and Answers** section provides four sets of exam-type questions on Beliefs in Society for you to try, together with some sample answers at A-grade and C-grade levels. Examiner's comments are included to show how marks are awarded at A2.

How to use this guide

To benefit most from this guide, you need to use different parts of it at different stages of your course. At the beginning of your study of Beliefs in Society, you should refer to this Introduction and have a look at the Content Guidance section. As you go through the topic, you should refer to the relevant part of the Content Guidance section to check on your progress and to ensure that you have understood the main concepts used. To gain full advantage from the Questions and Answers section, you should attempt to answer the questions progressively. Try to answer one or two sets of questions as you finish doing the topic of Beliefs in Society. This will help you to consolidate the knowledge you have gained and to organise your understanding of the topic in a systematic fashion. As you move into revision mode for the unit examination, attempt those questions that you have not done, as part of an active revision strategy.

To use the questions and answers effectively, you have to be honest and not look at the answers before you have attempted the question yourself. Study your chosen question carefully and then attempt to answer each part (or the whole question if it is an essay response) *without* looking first at the example answers provided. It is important that you work in this way — by comparing your answers with the specimen answers, you will understand what you might have done better and so improve your performance. When you have completed your answers, study the A-grade candidate's answers and identify where you might have made other links. Look carefully at the examiner's comments to see where you might have been able to make further improvements, giving particular thought to the different skills that you have to demonstrate. You should also look at the C-grade answers and, using the examiner's comments as a guide, rewrite them so that they would gain A-grade marks.

These activities are time-consuming and should not be attempted all at one go. Divide up the tasks you have to do into manageable chunks and complete the activities over a number of weeks. Keep in mind that you will need to have everything completed in good time for the examination. You will therefore need to know on what date the Unit 3 exam is to be held. You should then be able to fit these activities in with your other revision tasks.

In addition to using the questions to develop your examination skills, you could draw on the answers as a source of revision material. Reading through the A-grade candidate's answers should provide you with useful reminders of important sociological material. Remember, however, that in the exam you must answer the question that is on your paper — you should not try to reproduce the specimen answer.

The A2 specification

The aims of the A2 Sociology course are to enable you to:
- acquire knowledge and a critical understanding of contemporary social processes and social changes
- appreciate the significance of theoretical and conceptual issues in sociological debate
- understand and evaluate sociological methodology and a range of research methods through active involvement in the research process
- develop skills that enable individuals to focus on their personal identity, roles and responsibilities in society
- develop a lifelong interest in social issues

In addition, there should be an emphasis on contemporary society.

Examinable skills

A2 Sociology papers are designed to test certain defined skills. These skills are expressed as assessment objectives in the AQA specification. You will have been tested in these assessment objectives in your AS Sociology unit examinations, but the weighting for each of the two assessment objectives (AO1 and AO2) is different for the A2 Sociology specification. Over the two units of A2, the proportion of marks given to AO1 (knowledge and understanding) is just over 40% and for AO2 (application, analysis, interpretation and evaluation), it is about 58%. The effect of this is that, at A2, you have to be able to demonstrate more sophisticated skills of analysis and evaluation than at AS. You will be required to show a more critical, reflective and evaluative approach to methodological issues, to the nature of sociological enquiry and to sociological debates, drawing on a broad and diverse range of sources.

Unit 3 constitutes 20% of the total marks available for the whole of AS and A2, but the assessment objective weighting for Unit 3 is 40% for AO1 skills and 60% for AO2 skills. This shows the proportion of marks allocated to each of the two assessment objectives. Three-fifths of the 60 marks available in the Unit 3 examination are therefore awarded to the demonstration of AO2 skills and only two-fifths to AO1 skills.

Assessment objective 1 (AO1): knowledge and understanding

AO1 concerns the paired skills of knowledge and understanding. You have to demonstrate clearly to the examiners that you have appropriate, accurate knowledge and a good understanding of the sociological material in the topic you are studying. You will find an account of the basic knowledge required for Beliefs in Society in the Content Guidance section of this guide. The reason for bringing together knowledge and understanding is that it is not enough to be able to reproduce in the exam knowledge learned by rote. You must also be able to use this knowledge in a meaningful way to answer the specific question set. This includes the ability to select the most appropriate information from the range of knowledge that you have.

In addition, you have to demonstrate your knowledge and understanding of the **core themes** of the specification. These are:
- socialisation, culture and identity
- social differentiation, power and stratification

Aspects of these themes are dealt with in various elements of the AS and A2 courses. The themes therefore run through the whole of the course and this includes the topic of Beliefs in Society. You will see examples of where these themes are dealt with in the Content Guidance section of this guide.

Each topic in sociology, including Beliefs in Society, also has to cover what are called **integral elements**, that is, information and approaches that are central to sociology and that are found in all the topics studied at Advanced level. The integral elements cover:
- sociological theories, perspectives and methods
- the design and evaluation of research methods

Therefore, one of the demands of the AQA specification for AS and A2 Sociology is that you have a good knowledge and understanding of a range of sociological methods and sources and that, in particular, you understand the relationship between theory and methods. This includes the way that sociologists:

- acquire primary and secondary data through observation, asking questions and using documents
- analyse qualitative and quantitative data using appropriate concepts
- take into account factors influencing the design and conduct of sociological research
- are influenced by practical, ethical and theoretical considerations

The nature of sociological thought is concerned with both concepts and sociological theories. A requirement of the specification is that you make the links between these concepts and theories and the substantive area you have chosen to study — in this case, Beliefs in Society. The nature of sociological thought covers:

- social order, social control
- social change
- conflict and consensus
- social structure and social action
- the role of values
- the relationship between sociology and contemporary social policy

The final part of the AO1 skills requirement concerns the quality of written communication. This includes the ability to:

- use a style of writing appropriate for transmitting complex information
- use specialist vocabulary, such as sociological concepts, when appropriate
- use accurate spelling, punctuation and grammar to ensure that the meaning is clear and the text is legible

Assessment objective 2 (AO2): application, analysis, interpretation and evaluation

AO2 covers application, analysis, interpretation and evaluation. At A2 you will need to be more critical and evaluative than in the AS exams, as more marks are given to AO2 skills than to AO1 skills.

You will, therefore, need to:

- select appropriate pieces of sociological knowledge and arguments and distinguish between facts and opinion (**application**)
- break down sociological studies and debates into their component parts, i.e. concepts, perspective, method, findings, conclusion, strengths and weaknesses (**analysis**)
- examine material such as statistics, tables, graphs, research findings etc. to identify trends and establish their meaning and importance (**interpretation**)
- assess the relevance and importance of sociological studies and debates, conveying their strengths and weaknesses and coming to a conclusion about them (**evaluation**)

Evaluation is a particularly important skill at A2. In practice, this means that you should be asking questions such as, 'Why should I believe this?', 'What evidence is there for this viewpoint?', 'Are there any counter-arguments?' and 'Who says so?' for every piece of sociological research or approach that you come across. Try to develop the habit of evaluation as you go through your course. A good way to do this is to establish a minimum of two strengths and two weaknesses for every piece of research or every point of view or sociological perspective that you examine. It is even better if you can come to a conclusion about whether every item is convincing or not, with your conclusion backed by rational argument and solid sociological research.

As well as the above skills, AO2 includes the ability to:
- organise your arguments coherently
- display an understanding of theoretical debates in sociology
- marshal evidence to support arguments and any conclusions you make

Study skills and revision strategies

Study skills

As you go through your A2 course, you should seek to establish routines of study that will help you specifically with the exciting challenges of sociology. The first set of study skills, however, is basic to all your subjects:
- Develop a consistent way of taking notes, both from your teachers and from your reading. There are various techniques and types of shorthand you can try, but the important thing is to establish what works best for you and keep to it consistently.
- Review your notes at regular intervals.
- Produce reduced versions of your notes that will help you to revise later on.
- Practise doing examination questions on a regular basis.
- Read everything that your teacher asks you to and try to do some of your own reading as well, focusing on what particularly interests you about a topic.
- Use the internet independently but *carefully* to find out about contemporary examples and current developments in sociology.
- Keep to the regular homework pattern established by your teachers, handing in work when due, and reading carefully any comments made on your work.

The second set of study skills pertains to A-level Sociology in a more focused way:
- Try to read a quality newspaper every day or, failing that, at least a quality Sunday newspaper. Newspapers such as the *Guardian*, the *Independent*, *The Times* or the *Observer* are invaluable resources for a whole range of sociological topics. They are also useful for you to practise applying your sociological skills to contemporary news stories and for picking up examples to use in the examination. Use your school or local library as a source of these newspapers, or access them online.
- Use the internet when requested to do so and as often as you otherwise can. There are some excellent sites dedicated to A-level Sociology and more general sociological sites that will stretch your sociological imagination.

- Subscribe to *Sociology Review* and access back copies held by your school or college library. It is one of the best sources of contemporary sociological work in the areas you will be examined on.
- Watch television and films from a sociological point of view and try to apply appropriate concepts to the stories. The least it will do is drive your friends, parents and siblings mad.

Revision strategies

Here you should take note of the following points:

- Before you start your revision make sure that you are aware of what the awarding body — the AQA — specifies for the examination. Get yourself a copy of the specification, which is downloadable from the internet.
- Organise your revision by establishing a timetable for the 2 months before the examination — plan for all your subjects and also some free time for yourself. Use a website such as *Get Revising* (**http://getrevising.co.uk/**) to help you with this.
- Be active in your revision strategies — don't just sit there and read your notes. Try to do exercises and activities that test your AO2 skills.
- Practise 'real' exam questions as often as you can. Look at the answers in this unit guide and use them as exemplars and for improving your own performance.
- Take note of what your teachers tell you to do and do it — they are trying to help you, not make your life miserable.
- Organise your revision so that you are not trying to do it all in the few nights before the exam. You need to sleep well the night before.
- In the exam, divide your time appropriately for the number of marks and make sure that you attempt all parts of a question asked.

The unit examination

Beliefs in Society is a Unit 3 topic. The unit also contains the topics of Global Development, Mass Media and Power and Politics. It is unlikely that you will have covered more than one of these topics in your course, but, if you have, you must choose only *one* of the four sections on the examination paper. Beliefs in Society is Section A. It is worth 20% of the entire A-level qualification and is therefore an important component.

Within Section A, you have to answer question 1, which consists of two parts — 1 (a) and 1 (b). This is compulsory. There are then two essay questions and you must choose only one of these (question 2 or question 3).

Attached to question 1 will be a single item of source material. This is designed to help you by providing information on which you may draw to answer question 1 (a) and/or 1 (b). You should read this material carefully, *before* attempting to answer the questions. It may provide you with important clues in answering one or both of the parts. When one of the questions refers specifically to the source material ('Using Item A' or 'With reference to Item A and elsewhere'), you are *required* to make use of the source material. You should do this as obviously as possible to assist the marker in identifying where in your answer you have obeyed the instruction. For example, you might write:

'As Item A demonstrates...'

'The view in Item A suggests a functionalist approach is most useful...'

Timing and mark allocation

Unit 3 Section A questions are worth 60 marks in total, with 9 marks given to question 1 (a), 18 marks to question 1 (b) and 33 marks to either question 2 or question 3, depending on which you choose.

The division of marks between the elements you have to answer (9, 18 and 33) indicates the time that you should allocate to each element. As you have 1 hour and 30 minutes, you should devote roughly half of the time to question 2 or question 3 (about 50 minutes), about 20 minutes to question 1 (b) and about 10 minutes to question 1 (a), leaving 5 minutes for reading through the item of source material and 5 minutes' reviewing at the end.

As we have seen, 40% of the marks in Unit 3 as a whole are given to AO1 skills and 60% to AO2 skills. There is some variation within this, however. In questions 2 or 3, the balance of AO1 and AO2 marks is nearly equal — 15 marks for AO1 and 18 marks for AO2. In question 1 (parts (a) and (b)), AO2 marks are in the majority. For question 1 (a), AO1 is given 3 marks and AO2 6 marks. For question 1 (b), AO1 is given 6 marks and AO2 12 marks. A further complication is that, in the longer essay questions (questions 2 or 3), the AO2 marks are subdivided equally between AO2 (a), interpretation and application and AO2 (b), analysis and evaluation, with 9 marks for each.

The important thing to note in all this is that the skills of interpretation, application, analysis and evaluation are more important in A2 examinations than they are at AS, and therefore you must take care to demonstrate them. Pay particular attention to the wording of questions, which provides you with clues as to the particular skills being asked for. Remember also that you need to provide evidence of knowledge and understanding of material from Beliefs in Society, so do not neglect this skill either.

For the range of issues that may be examined in Unit 3, see the next section of this guide, Content Guidance.

Content Guidance

This section is intended to show you the major issues and themes covered in **Beliefs in Society** and the main points of evaluation that have been made about them. We have also identified the key concepts and key writers in each area. These are offered as guidance only. The points included are not exhaustive — you may raise other perfectly legitimate points. You will find many other concepts and studies that are relevant to your exploration of Beliefs in Society, including religion. The main studies and arguments in religion are well rehearsed in all the major textbooks, so you should have no trouble finding these out. Your teacher will also give you other studies during your course. The main magazine for A-level sociologists (*Sociology Review*) has repeatedly focused on the issues of religion, and so back copies, available from your school or college library, will be a useful source of information. It is always a good idea to read some original research on a particular topic and religion is full of interesting and accessible books and articles. If these are not available to you, most of the textbooks have good accounts of relevant ideas and arguments.

The content of the AQA A2 topic of Beliefs in Society falls into five main areas:
- theories of religion and belief
- the role of religion in societies and its relationship to social change and stability
- forms of religious organisation, including cults, sects, denominations, churches and New Age movements
- the relationship between social groups, religious beliefs and practices and religious/spiritual organisations
- the secularisation debate, in a global context

The topic is designed to give you a comprehensive understanding of the importance of these areas in contemporary and past societies. You are expected to be familiar with the major sociological explanations of religion and belief, in terms of their functions for society and for individuals. This will include the classical sociologists' views on religion, which they all thought was central to understanding the operation of societies, as well as more recent approaches such as postmodernism. There were strong differences of opinion among the classical sociologists as to whether religion brought people together or kept them apart, and whether it was a force for change or stability. You will also need to be familiar with the range of different religious organisations that exist and their relationship to various social groups. Last, one of the main debates in the sociology of religion is the continued importance of religion in contemporary societies and the contradictory evidence about the development of a secular society. This debate occurs at three levels — society, religious practices and individual consciousness.

Theories of religion

Definitions

Key ideas

- Definitions are important because they decide what should be examined as a religious phenomenon and what should not.
- Inclusivist definitions include many phenomena that might seem controversial, such as magic, or even non-religious beliefs, such as communism.
- Exclusivist definitions exclude phenomena that do not make reference to a supernatural being and limit what can be defined as religious.
- Functional definitions of religion focus on the role that a religious phenomenon performs for society as a whole, such as acting as a unifying force.
- Substantive definitions refer to a defining characteristic, such as a belief in God, as the distinctive feature of religion.
- Inclusivist definitions are 'essentialist', that is, they take the position that religious belief and activity is a necessary feature of the human condition, although it may take many forms.
- Exclusivist definitions are 'non-essentialist', accepting that there may be a decline or growth in religious activity at different historical stages.
- Quasi-religions have a 'this world' orientation and can focus on sport, shopping, rock, television personalities etc.
- The definition adopted leads the sociologist to ask different questions about the scale and importance of religious belief and activity in society, and possibly to reach different conclusions.
- Religions can be seen as a form of ideology, serving the interests of a particular social group.

Evaluation

- + Inclusivist-functionalist definitions allow the sociologist to investigate a wide range of historical and contemporary practices as 'religious', including humanism and psychoanalysis, because these are concerned with the 'ultimate problems' that confront all human beings.
- + Exclusivist-substantive definitions allow the sociologist to examine only those social phenomena that are commonsensically recognised as expressions of religious feeling.
- + Both approaches are attempting to identify what can be 'religious' in order to form a field of study with definite boundaries.
- − Inclusivist-functional definitions are drawn so wide that they make the idea of a specifically religious sphere of activity difficult to maintain — everything can be seen as 'religious'.
- − Exclusivist-substantive definitions limit what can be seen as religious and lead inevitably to the idea that religious observance has declined in importance, as its manifestation changes in society.

- Both approaches are actually linked to ideological positions that are associated with either supporting or undermining religious belief.

Key concepts

inclusivism, exclusivism, functionalism, essentialism, transcendence

Key thinkers

Durkheim, Weber, Bellah, Yinger, Robertson, Hunt

Durkheim

Key ideas

- Durkheim started from the position that social existence was only possible through the belief in shared ideas.
- He offered a functionalist definition of religion, as being 'beliefs and practices which unite into one single moral community called a Church'.
- Religion was therefore an essential part of the 'conscience collective', or the shared ideas that make social life possible.
- These shared ideas constituted the fundamental notions of time, space, causation and relationships that allow humankind to think logically.
- He distinguished between the 'profane' and the 'sacred', the former being everyday life and the latter constituting things set apart and forbidden.
- He drew these ideas from a study of the totemic religions of the Australian aborigines, in which the totem worshipped was a representation of the clan.
- The totem also symbolised society and the collective rituals of religion. In this sense it was a restatement of the importance of social bonds.
- Religion therefore acted to bind individuals to society, allowing them to understand and enact correct social relations between individuals, through the shared values of religious belief.
- Religion also regulated behaviour so that social life became possible without selfish individualism getting in the way.

Evaluation

+ Durkheim offered a functional explanation in which religion is given a dominant role in social cohesion.
+ He identified a moral dimension to the nature of social relationships, based on religious ideas.
+ He explained the existence of religion in terms of its rituals rather than its theological ideas.
- Durkheim ignored the importance of individual religious experience.
- He had a static view of religion; for example, he did not attempt to explain the rise of new religions or religious leaders.
- The practices of primitive religions do not explain the workings of religion in a complex, religiously diverse modern society.

Key concepts
conscience collective, sacred, profane, totems, representation

Key thinkers
Durkheim, Eister

Weber and Weberian approaches

Key ideas

- Weber believed that ideas, including religious ideas, had an independent effect on social and economic change.
- To demonstrate this, he examined the relationship between new religious ideas and the development of the capitalist system of production.
- Specifically he argued that the ethical orientation of Calvinist Protestants led to practices that gave impetus to capitalist modes of production — the 'spirit of capitalism'.
- Catholic culture was portrayed as being concerned with conspicuous consumption, whereas Protestantism encouraged a frugal frame of mind in which income was ploughed back into production rather than spent on luxuries.
- There was thus an 'elective affinity' between the Protestant ethic and the spirit of capitalism; the Protestant ethic was not the sole causal relationship, but an important factor.
- The ideas of Calvinism produced a particular personality trait that acted out patterns of conduct conducive to the development of capitalism.
- Weber also examined other religions to see if there were reasons why they did not lead to the development of capitalist modes of behaviour.
- Confucianism stressed adjustment to the world. By contrast, the uncertainty of Calvinism had the unintended consequence of leading believers to see worldly success as a sign of God's favour.
- Bellah argued that the relationship between religion and economics is indirect, operating through the political structure, rather than direct.
- Wertheim argued that all ideas, for example scientific thought, have a transformative capacity, not just religious ones.

Evaluation

+ Weber stressed the importance of ideas as causal factors in social developments, rejecting economic determinism.
+ He sought to explain social change as a complex interplay of forces, but in which there are decisive points in history that can be identified through sociological analysis.
+ Weber's argument offers a cross-cultural approach to social change, using data from a number of societies to explore a particular hypothesis and come to a conclusion.
− Weber did not demonstrate how strongly individual entrepreneurs held their religious beliefs and therefore whether these affected their patterns of behaviour.

- It has been claimed that the connection between religion and economics has been over-stressed, with many other factors suggested as the cause of capitalism.
- It has been argued that it was not the religious belief of the Calvinists that was important for the development of capitalism but their marginal position in a Catholic society that led them to strive for wealth.

Key concepts

Calvinistic Protestantism, spirit of capitalism, elective affinity, transformative capacity, cross-culturalism

Key thinkers

Weber, Tawney, Wertheim, Sombart

Marx

Key ideas

- Marx saw religion as an aspect of ideology, rather than as important in its own right.
- It was an important element in the 'false consciousness' of the workers and of the bourgeoisie, in that neither had a real appreciation of their position as pawns of the system.
- For the workers, religion was one way in which their alienation was alleviated, focusing their attention on the rewards of the next world rather than the misery of this one.
- However, religion also represented the workers' yearning for a better world, their hopes for a future better than their present situation.
- For the bourgeoisie, religion was a cloak of respectability behind which they relentlessly pursued profit at the expense of the workers.
- Protestantism, with its emphasis on the 'abstract individual' facing his or her maker alone, allowed the bourgeoisie to treat their workers not as men or women but as commodities to be bought and sold.
- Both bourgeoisie and proletariat were subject to the impersonal forces of capitalism, which destroyed and favoured individuals in an apparently random fashion for which no religion could compensate.
- Kautsky argued that it was the development of capitalism that led to the creation of Protestant ideas, to justify the economic activities of the bourgeoisie.

Evaluation

+ The phenomenon of religion is seen by Marxism as being determined by the economic base, so giving primary importance to economic activity rather than ideas.
+ The positions of both proletariat and bourgeoisie are explained in terms of the role of religion in an inhumane system.
+ Religion is a delusion of the mind, designed to resign individuals to their lot.

- Marxism dismisses the reality of sincere religious feelings that individuals experience.
- It is monocausal, explaining religion purely as an epiphenomenon of the economic system.
- Religion has an impact on social groups other than just social classes, such as ethnic groups, but these are not addressed.

Key concepts

alienation, bourgeoisie, proletariat, false consciousness

Key thinkers

Marx, Feuerbach, Kautsky

Functionalism

Key ideas

- Though drawn from Durkheim, functionalist thought on religion differs from Durkheim's views in certain crucial respects.
- Totemism is not a set of unified practices, as envisaged by Durkheim, but ranges from very complex formulations to trivial phenomena like totem poles.
- Totemism can also be seen not as the relation of the individual to the social world, but as expressing the individual's relationship to the natural world (Levi-Strauss).
- An alternative functionalist theory was put forward by Malinowski, who saw religion as the response of individuals to the uncertainty of the world, fulfilling an emotional need for security.
- Religion can function to bind individuals together in the face of the death of one member of a group, through the comfort of collective rituals.
- Religion therefore makes a unique contribution to social integration.
- Any decline in religious belief or practice leads to increased social disorganisation.
- Religion, therefore, is an essential feature of all successful societies.
- It is the only aspect of human experience that can grasp the non-empirical, and as such is a necessary basis for human action.

Evaluation

+ Functionalism insists on looking at the social dimension rather than the individual for an explanation of religion.
+ By emphasising the importance of religion in social integration, it answers the Hobbesian 'problem of order' of how we can live together peacefully.
+ It deals with the supernatural as a 'real' phenomenon of subjective experience.
- Many societies seem to exist without a unifying religion in the conventional sense.
- Functionalism asserts rather than explains how religion reinforces common values, especially in multireligious societies.
- Religious participation can exist without any corresponding strong religious belief.

totemism, social integration, the supernatural, social disorganisation

Durkheim, Radcliffe-Brown, Levi-Strauss, Malinowski, Davis, Parsons, Bellah

Interactionism

Key ideas

- Phenomenologists focus on the states of consciousness of individuals, including their religious consciousness, as they live out their everyday lives in the Lebenswelt.
- Religion is established by human enterprise or actions, in which objects or beings are given awesome power, standing apart from, but related to, the existence of humanity.
- This sacred dimension is the opposite of the chaos that confronts individuals as they try to make sense of their lives.
- Religion therefore gives us ultimate meanings, making the universe manageable by reducing it to a human-centred enterprise, in which we gain significance in the cosmic order.
- A higher plane of existence is indicated by many aspects of human experience — when we discover order in our lives, from the joy of play, from hope, from events experienced as evil, from humour.
- Religion is therefore about cognition, providing us all with the categories and concepts needed to make sense of the world.
- We all share these existential concerns (what is life, death, joy, suffering etc.) and all therefore have religiosity — a sense of the supernatural.
- As an individual phenomenon, contemporary religion has many of the features of a supermarket, in which individuals are free to choose or change according to personal inclination.

+ Interactionists take religious feeling and sensibility as a 'real' phenomenon experienced by people, rather than as a false consciousness.
+ Interactionism deals with the issue of 'ultimate meaning' rather than taking a strictly materialist approach.
+ It takes religion as an everyday activity rather than at the level of the institution.
- Interactionists place too much emphasis on the subjective meaning of religion, ignoring its power and influence on the institutional level, for example.
- Phenomenological approaches suffer from 'cognitive reductionism', overemphasising the rational/thoughtful aspects of religion, against its emotional appeal.
- Interactionism assumes that we all have a measure of religious feeling that must be fulfilled, when, in fact, religious sensibility can be shown to be distributed according to social class.

Lebenswelt, everyday world, spiritual supermarket, cognitive reductionism

Berger, Berger and Luckmann, Turner, Bibby, Beckford

Postmodernism

Key ideas

- With the collapse of religious certainty represented by the 'sacred canopy' of a universally accepted religion, individuals have to seek their own 'meaning-routes' through the wealth of religious choices on offer.
- As the old religious certainties fade, new forms of religious connectedness are made between individuals, either referring back to certainty or rejecting it in favour of the individual quest for truth.
- In a network society, where flows of power, wealth and information are beyond individual control, individuals may turn to the power of religious identity to try to exercise some control over their situation.
- As religion becomes 'à la carte', the choice is between forms of haute cuisine (traditional religion) and McDonaldisation (standardised but bland religious ideas).
- In a postmodern world of endless choice, religious fundamentalism is not a 'throwback' but a rational response to 'choice overload', where the individual has to make myriad choices not only of consumer products, but also between ideas and values.
- The media are a crucial aspect of postmodern religion, with some sociologists seeing the internet as a new metaphor for the nature of God, being decentralised and dispersed (Turkle).
- As religion becomes packaged as a commodity in the market place, it becomes Disneyfied, that is, trivial and crowd-pleasing.
- Globalisation trends are reflected in the emergence of new religious movements that look for a unifying and common religious culture under such names as Gaia or planetary theology.

+ Postmodernism seeks to explain the explosion of religious sects and cults in contemporary capitalist societies.
+ It locates movements such as fundamentalism and planetary ecology within the conditions of contemporary postmodern living.
+ It emphasises the importance of the hyper-reality of the media in contemporary religious life.
- It overemphasises the degree to which the old certainties have collapsed and we are faced with genuine choices.
- Fundamentalism can be seen as a reactionary response to modernism, rather than a postmodern response to choice.

– Postmodernism denies the serious way in which individuals approach religion in favour of a 'playful' perspective.

> **Key concepts**

network society, 'à la carte' religion, choice overload, McDonaldisation, Disneyfication

> **Key thinkers**

Bauman, Castells, Limieux, Heelas, Turkle, Lyon

The role of religion

As a unifying force

Key ideas

- Where there is a 'sacred canopy' of a universal religion in a society, it can act as a force for solidarity.
- A common religion offers a set of values that shapes behaviour in a specific way, so that all are agreed on appropriate conduct.
- This can lead to a form of mechanistic solidarity in society, in which there is an identification through sameness, based on religious belief.
- Secular formations, such as the monarchy, use religious symbolism to reinforce their claim to represent the nation and act as a focus of loyalty.
- In a global society of mass migrations, religion can act as a unifying force for disparate populations; for example when an allegiance to Islam assists marginal populations to carve out an identity.
- The importance of Christianity in the United States is that it acts as a unifier of a mainly immigrant society, despite differences in the particular form of Christianity adopted.
- Diasporic populations, such as the Jews, use religion as a marker for identity, despite surface differences between forms of the religion, such as Orthodox or liberal or reform Judaism.
- In divided societies, such as Ireland, religion can act as a signifier, uniting distinct populations in opposition to the 'Other'.
- Secular ideologies have sought to replace religion as a unifying force. Communism, for example, took on many aspects of religion, such as the 'saints' of Marx, Engels and Lenin.

> **Evaluation**

+ This view emphasises the positive aspects of religion, showing it as a force for integration, identity and solidarity.
+ It explains the persistence of religious differences in populations characterised by migration.

+ It focuses on the common elements that members of a religion share, through an acceptance of shared ideas and allegiances.
– The idea of a unifying religious force is more appropriate for historical societies than for contemporary ones.
– The 'sacred canopy' idea overestimates the degree of real loyalty to and belief in an overarching religion, such as Catholicism in medieval Europe, as individuals often only pay lip-service to such beliefs.
– The history of religion suggests that it is more significant for its ability to divide people than unite them, as in religious wars or the contemporary Middle East.

Key concepts
integration, sacred canopy, diaspora, global society

Key thinkers
Durkheim, Shils, Parsons, Bellah

As a source of conflict

Key ideas

- Strong faith in a particular religion often involves a deep belief in the 'wrongness' of other religious forms, expressed in such terms as heresy, abomination and false belief.
- Religion can generate strong collective feelings that function to separate out often minority groups from mainstream society, so that conflict occurs over the allocation of resources to particular religious segments of the community.
- Religious allegiance often parallels other social divisions, particularly of class and ethnicity, compounding the potential for misunderstanding and conflict.
- Many religious faiths have a powerful 'missionary' zeal associated with them, in which adherents are called upon to proselytise (convert) the non-believer, by force if necessary.
- Historically and in contemporary politics, many wars have been and are fought in the name of religion; for example, the conflict in the Middle East and the 'war against terrorism' have a religious dimension to them.
- Where religions have an eschatological dimension (a belief in the end of the world), believers may be careless of their own earthly lives and strive for immortality through violent actions against those they identify as the religious enemy.
- Marxists claim that religious conflicts mask economic conflicts and therefore act as a smokescreen for the exploitation of the have-nots by the haves.
- Where there is a strong 'state' religion, in which one form of religious belief is given privileges by the state over all others, members of other religions may suffer discrimination or disadvantage; for example, in Great Britain a Roman Catholic cannot legally become the monarch.
- Religion is often mixed up with cultural struggles over what is correct behaviour and beliefs for individuals, as evidenced in the fatwa against Salman Rushdie.

- Many contemporary believers feel threatened by secular forces undermining their core beliefs, such as the 'culture war' in the USA over gay marriage.

Evaluation

+ This view focuses on the history of religions rather than the idealism of their theology or ideology.
+ It suggests that religions have a 'dark side' and are not all peace and love to humankind.
+ It directs attention to the consequences of religious discrimination and the disadvantages that members of particular faiths may experience in society.
− It downplays the real good that religions have achieved in the world, in terms of both religious organisations and individual believers.
− It assumes that adherents to different religions are inevitably drawn into conflict through their religious differences.
− It ignores movements, such as ecumenicalism, that seek to forge bridges not just within different sections of the same world religions, but between members of all faiths.

Key concepts

fundamentalism, religion as a smokescreen, exclusivist religion

Key thinkers

Marx, Kepel, Wallis, Bromley and Shupe

As a conservative force

Key ideas

- The notion of religion as a conservative force is based on the links in many societies between the state and a specific religion, where there are pervasive political, social and economic connections between high-ranking members of the religion and political personalities.
- It is related to functionalist ideas that religion serves to integrate individuals into a dominant status quo, but goes further in arguing that religion seeks to defend political and social arrangements as they are.
- Religion thus has an important legitimising function for many regimes. For example, some claim that Methodism, because of its conservative nature, was the main reason why the working classes did not revolt in nineteenth-century Britain.
- The classic example of the fusion of religious and political power is in the Vatican State, where the Papacy is both a temporal and a spiritual phenomenon.
- The involvement of Evangelical Christians in right-wing politics in the United States is seen as one of the main manifestations of contemporary religious conservatism.
- This identification of religion with the status quo has led in some instances to the dominant religion of a society being associated with authoritarian and occasionally violent political regimes, such as in the case of Pinochet's Chile.

- The Iranian revolution of Ayatollah Khomenei can be seen either as a conservative revolution in defence of traditional Islamic values or as a reactionary movement against the modernisation and Westernisation of Iran by the Shah.
- There is also a wider sense in which religion can be seen as a conservative force, in that many long-established religions act in defence of 'traditional' values and ways of behaving and are often critical of modernising tendencies, such as Taliban rule in Afghanistan.
- The traditional conservative values of many religions seem to conflict with modern and postmodern ways of living, but are also powerful attractions to many individuals who are bemused by the lack of certainty in their lives.
- Many individuals are able to adhere to the conservative message of their religious beliefs while acting in ways that are contrary to them. Many Roman Catholics, for example, practise birth control, which is barred by the Catholic church.
- Secular ideologies can also act as a conservative force, even when apparently 'revolutionary', once their adherents have taken power; for example, the USSR before the downfall of communism.

Evaluation

+ This view places an emphasis on tradition and continuity that has a wide appeal in conditions of change.
+ It locates allegiance to a particular state in a religious context, thus legitimising and securing it against discontent and rebellion.
+ It identifies values that seem to have endured for many years and act as a call to 'correct behaviour'.
- The conservative leanings of many religious personalities have led to their defence of some unpleasant regimes that have little respect for human rights.
- Unquestioning support for the way things have always been impedes progress in many spheres of social life, for example in women's rights.
- Values that are unchanging are likely to conflict with changing social conditions and lead to misery for individuals as they juggle their beliefs and their way of life.

Key concepts

universal church, religious reaction, legitimation, anti-modernity, Westernisation

Key thinkers

Parsons, Troeltsch, Yinger, Halevy

As a source of change

Key ideas

- Drawn from the work of Weber, this approach emphasises the role of religion in stimulating social, political or economic change through the evolution of new religious ideas.

- It is associated with the thesis of the 'spirit of capitalism', in which the emergence of Calvinism acted as a spur to the development of capitalist modes of behaviour that transformed feudal societies.
- This view of religions is based on the idea that they contain within them the potential for both reactionary and radical actions, and therefore religious believers can be mobilised for progressive causes.
- Liberation theology of the 1960s and 1970s is seen as an example of the 'commitment to the poor' by worker-priests and nuns in Latin America, which led many grass-root leaders of the Roman Catholic church to involve themselves in radical and even revolutionary movements.
- With an emphasis on justice, many religious movements, such as the World Council of Churches, supported the anti-apartheid movement in South Africa.
- Where religion forms an oppositional focus to repressive regimes, it can be used for political change, even where it is violent, such as in the Iranian revolution.
- Religious organisations also formed the basis of many anti-colonial movements in Africa, such as Alice Lenshina's Church in Zambia, where the mix of Christian and traditional religious forms was tried to establish an authentic African voice.
- Religion also formed the core of resistance of native Americans to encroachment by white society during the 'Ghost Dances' in the late nineteenth century.
- Scientific ideas have been, and continue to be, a massive source of change in societies, for example the growth of the internet or the potential of stem cell research to change individual destiny.

Evaluation

- \+ This approach acknowledges the contradictory potential of religion for both conservative and radical ends.
- \+ It develops a historical perspective in understanding the nature of religion as a tool of the oppressed to resist their condition.
- \+ It offers a positive view of religion's role in society, stressing its potential for achieving essential changes needed to promote values, such as justice, which are both secular and religious.
- − It tends to overestimate the success of religious movements in promoting social change, as in Latin America where liberation theology has been essentially neutralised.
- − It sees social change as an end in its own right, without examining the consequences of such change for the people it is supposed to assist, for example justifying repressive regimes that might emerge as a result.
- − It downplays other forces for social change in favour of religion, negating economic and political movements such as the anti-colonial movement.

Key concepts

mobilisation, commitment to the poor, liberation theology

Key thinkers

Weber, Wilson, Debray, Mooney

Religious organisations

Church and sect

Key ideas

- A fundamental distinction in Christian religious organisations is the difference between church and sect as elaborated by Troeltsch.
- Both churches and sects believe that only their members will gain salvation and that the adherents of other organisations or religions will not be in a 'state of grace'.
- Churches believe that salvation is given in a mystical manner as an infant is received through baptism into the pre-existing church ('salvation through grace'). The individual is therefore born into the church, experiencing it as an objective reality with a long tradition.
- Sects believe that salvation depends upon the rational assent of the adult individual to believe in a personal God and to live in a voluntary community of 'saints', made up of the other believers ('salvation through faith').
- Churches are positive in their attitudes towards the established social order, often having formal links with the state. In some cases their higher personnel are drawn from the upper classes.
- Sects are more associated with lower social classes, separate from the establishment, and have a more tense relationship with the state, sometimes being in strong opposition to the secular order.
- Churches develop ideologies to defend and legitimate the status quo, such as the divine right of kings in monarchical societies. These ideologies may become outdated, but are retained as part of the tradition of the church.
- Sects tend not to look to the past but to live in the present, 'living the life' of faith, with their values constantly being renewed as a result of their everyday experiences of God's presence.
- Churches and sects should not be seen only in uniform terms, nor as resistant to change. Churches have within them enthusiastic and evangelical elements, while sects are subject to routinisation and also have a formal element.

Evaluation

- + This distinction identifies key respects in which religious organisations may differ.
- + It is a useful tool to use when beginning to analyse the behaviour and ideas of religious organisations.
- + It focuses on the social dimension of religious organisations, examining their relationship with social hierarchies.
- − The distinction is more appropriate to an earlier period of history, when, during the Reformation, Europeans were divided between a Catholic church and oppositional Protestant sects.
- − It does not take account of the dynamics of religious organisations, which can change their forms over time, with churches becoming more sect-like and vice versa.

– Sects are less persecuted in contemporary Western societies and may therefore
    have lost their antipathy to the state.

Key concepts

legitimation, opposition, salvation through grace, salvation through faith, routinisation

Key thinkers

Weber, Troeltsch, Barker

Denominations and cults

Key ideas

- Denominations were described by Niebuhr as 'a compromise between Christianity
  and the world' to indicate that they were distinctive from and somewhere between
  the formalism of churches and the inspirationalism of sects.
- Originally sect-like in their religious devotion, as the second generation was born
  they took on more of the attributes of churches.
- The crucial issue that turned some sects towards more routinised forms of worship
  was that of baptising infants. While sects emphasised adult baptism, some
  members wanted their children to be brought up in the organisation and used
  infant baptism as a sign of their commitment. This turned them to more church-
  like practices, which came to be associated with denominations.
- The growing wealth of sect members, as they lived frugal and productive lives in
  their faith, eventually contributed to the development of many sects into more
  formal denominations.
- However, there was no inevitability in this process. Wealthy sects could retain
  their sect-like character or renew their enthusiasm rather than become routinised.
- Denominations are distinct from sects and churches in their non-universalist
  approach; that is, they accept that there are other ways to salvation than just
  through membership of their specific organisation.
- A further complication of any typology is the existence of cults.
- Cults were originally a private form of religion, usually with a mystic dimension.
- 'Cult' is widely used now to indicate secretive and domineering sect-like organisations that may operate with manipulative mind-control techniques and have a
  highly exclusivist agenda, cutting off adherents from family non-believers.
- Wallis classifies churches, sects, denominations and cults according to whether
  the wider world sees them as being respectable (church and denomination) or
  deviant (sects and cults), as well as whether they see themselves as being the only
  road to salvation (church and sect) or not (denomination and cult).

Evaluation

  + These categories add to our understanding of the complexity of types of religious
    organisation.
  + They emphasise processes of change in the form of religious organisations and stress
    the importance of social development in the evolution of any specific organisation.

+ The concept of the 'cult' allows an exploration of some of the more negative aspects of religious organisations.
− Not all sects believe in the values of thrift. Therefore, there is no necessary process of becoming wealthy and upwardly mobile, thus creating the impetus towards a denomination.
− Many sects, for example the Jehovah's Witnesses, far from being led by charismatic and inspirational leaders, are very bureaucratic, so routinisation cannot be claimed as a feature of becoming a denomination.
− The idea of the cult creates a stereotype of religious organisations that can be used to criticise the activities of any of them.

Key concepts
formalism, inspirationalism, baptism, non-universalism, mysticism

Key thinkers
Niebuhr, von Weise, Wallis

More complex views of religious organisation

Key ideas

- The range of religious organisations is much larger than the four-fold divisions of church, sect, denomination and cult suggested by many typologies.
- In addition, the role of any religious organisation cannot be said to be either conservative or radical at all times, but varies according to which level of the organisation is examined, the cultural and historical context within which it operates, as well as the nature of its beliefs.
- 'Universal church' refers to a dominant religious form that is cross-national and operates independently of individual political units. An example is Roman Catholicism before the Reformation.
- An ecclesia refers to a religion that is identifiable as the state religion of a specific nation-state, such as Shia Islam in Iran.
- An established sect refers to a long-lived sect that has made an accommodation with the state over most issues, but remains opposed to the state on certain specifics. The pacifism of the Quaker movement is an example.
- Sects can take many forms and can be classified according to their attitude towards the secular world. They may accept it as a something to be lived with and celebrated, or avoid the world completely, or be actively opposed and hostile to the secular powers.
- Sects can be further divided into many different types, from the conversionist, evangelical, fundamentalist sects to thaumaturgical sects that seek contact with a spirit world.

- The relationship of any religious organisation to the world is complex, and each empirical example needs to be examined separately rather than stereotypically.

Evaluation

+ These complex typologies offer a more complete understanding of the nature of religious organisations.
+ They put forward a more dynamic view of the way that religious organisations operate in the world.
+ They suggest that religious organisations are subject to processes of change, as well as rooted in tradition.
− All these typologies can be criticised for focusing mainly on Christian organisations and ignoring or downplaying the other major world religions.
− Complex typologies can become so convoluted that they cease to have any explanatory power.
− The examples used to support particular typologies can often be based on a stereotypical view of the real religious life of organisations.

Key concepts

universal church, ecclesia, established sect, acceptance, aggression, avoidance

Key thinkers

Yinger, Wilson, Maguire

New Religious Movements

Key ideas

- 'New Religious Movements'(NRMs) is a term used to describe the many forms of religious groups that have emerged throughout the world, separate from the traditional forms of world religions, but often related to them.
- World-rejecting NRMs, such as Krishna Consciousness, are inward-looking and strict organisations that tend to avoid contact with outsiders as far as possible, in the search for spiritual enlightenment.
- World-affirming NRMs, such as Scientology, see success in the secular world as one of the aims of their spiritual journey within it.
- World-accommodating NRMs, such as Neo-Pentecostalism, are outward-looking, tolerant and charismatic movements.
- Some NRMs are accused of using brain-washing techniques and isolation of members from their families as a means of control, and can be associated with a charismatic leader, at whose command members will even take their own life.
- NRMs are believed to emerge during times of social change and are often seen as perfect for the postmodern era with its loss of certainty, in offering those in search of answers a 'true' account of the world.
- NRMs are said to offer recruits success in careers, improved health and self-development and 'authentic' religious experience, through 'client cults' and 'self-religions'.

- NRMs are often difficult to leave, partly because of the psychological investment that has been made in them, but also because the usual social ties may have been cut and continuing members may be hostile to the leaver.
- There has been much media attention on the 'doomsday' NRMs, whose members engage in acts of suicide (Jonesville) or terror (Aum Shinrikyo).
- A particular form of NRM is the political coalition of fundamentalist Christian groups in the United States (New Christian Right), which seek to impose their beliefs on the rest of society by influencing the president.
- New Age Movements, such as paganism, Gaia and astrology, are also seen as a form of alternative NRM, with a focus on inner spirituality, the environment, and forms of spiritualism and Eastern mysticism.

Evaluation

+ 'New Religious Movement', as a wider term than sect or cult, is a more appropriate way of defining the many religious groups that emerged in the latter part of the twentieth century.
+ NRMs have introduced a revival of religious feeling and devotion in many societies, and have attracted those who might otherwise be turned off from mainstream religion.
+ NRMs have had a positive effect on the mainstream Christian church in introducing charismatic behaviour and worship into traditional congregations.
− There is wide variation in NRMs, and many do not fit easily into the various categories proposed, nor do they emerge only in times of instability.
− NRMs are stereotyped as being 'dangerous' and controlling, when they may offer members reassurance and control over their own lives.
− NRMs are nothing new, as there have always been subterranean religious forms. However, in the past they were more likely to be criticised or even suppressed for being heretical.

Key concepts

world-affirming, world-rejecting, world-accommodating, charismatic, New Age, New Christian Right, client cults

Key thinkers

Wallis, Barker, Beckford, Davie, Bruce, Heelas

Religion and social groups
Religion and class

Key ideas

- From a Marxist perspective, religion has been seen as functioning as an ideology in defence of the interests of the dominant social class in society.

- Interest theorists argue that religious ideas are a weapon in the struggle for advantage between different social groups and a mask for real social and economic conflicts.
- Strain theorists argue that religions emerge as a result of social dislocation and personal tensions and function to resolve these tensions (catharsis) in ways that are advantageous to those who adhere to them, from providing a scapegoat for unpleasant events in symbolic evil to legitimating strain in terms of a higher being. The strains that may be resolved by religion are not only economic, but also social (in terms of lack of power or esteem), organismic (mental or physical impairment), psychic (anomie) and ethical (dissatisfaction with society's values).
- At the base of these theories is the fact that different social classes profess allegiance to different forms of religion, even within a broad world religion; for example, Shia Islam draws recruits mainly from among the poorer sections of Afghanistan.
- In Great Britain, the Church of England is dominated by a middle-class membership as it fails to recruit among the urbanised working classes.
- Some Protestant denominations, as well as Islam, Sikhism and Hinduism, find strong support in the working classes.
- Sects are sometimes seen as recruiting mainly from the disadvantaged in society, as they seek to resolve the tensions such people experience.
- Central to the appeal of religions are their 'theodices of good and ill fortune', that is the explanations for suffering or success, that legitimate the position of those who experience either.
- Religion is, therefore, a consequence of 'compensators' — the belief that reward for living a 'good life' will be obtained in the future, either on earth or in some form of heaven.

Evaluation

+ There is a class basis for many religious organisations and this has been explained through concepts such as compensators.
+ There is a link between world-affirming sects and the advantaged in society, and world-rejecting sects and the poor. This shows the importance of exploring the class nature of NRMs.
+ There are strong religious feelings among all social classes that express themselves in different ways and in different organisations.
– Sects are not just havens for the poor and dissatisfied, but also recruit from the rich and those who seemingly have everything.
– The statistical link between class and different types of sect is uncertain, especially because there are so few members of sects and cults.
– The appeal of religion is not universal among social classes and most individuals do not formally align to any religious organisation in contemporary Britain.

Key concepts

ideology, catharsis, solidarity, compensators

Key thinkers

Geertz, Glock and Stark, Stark and Bainbridge, Voas, Wallis

Religion and gender

Key ideas

- Many ancient religions had strong female images in the form of goddesses, but these have mainly been supplanted by male-dominated monotheistic religions such as Judaism, Christianity and Islam.
- The major religions therefore tend to privilege maleness in their theology, beliefs and practices.
- Where women are represented in religious beliefs, they tend to be in a submissive role or as agents of evil or temptation.
- Religious organisations are mainly male-led, especially at the higher levels, with the position of priest being barred to females in some major religions.
- Where females are allowed to take positions of authority or sacramental roles, it is only after long and protracted struggles by female (and male) adherents.
- Many religions seek to restrict the behaviour of women, emphasising modesty and submission to male authority. This can have a physical expression in the separation of male and female worshippers during religious services.
- Religions are often hostile to overt sexuality and see the control of women as essential to control the libido.
- Debates over the role of women in religion are seen as an argument between 'modernisers' and 'traditionalists', with the former often accused of being secular contaminators of 'pure' forms of religion.
- Outward religious forms for women are often presented in Western societies as symbolic of the 'Other', for example the wearing of the veil (hijab) by Muslim women.
- Yet, in many religions, women form the majority of regular attenders at services.
- In science, women's role in discovery has often been ignored or downplayed, such as Rosalind Franklin's contribution to the discovery of DNA.
- In New Age movements, a gender divide can be identified in the types of movements women and men are attracted to, with women favouring areas such as complementary medicine and men leaning towards parapsychology.

Evaluation

+ Women and men are claimed to have different natures and therefore the different roles within religion for men and women are 'natural'.
+ Religious recognition of the differences between men and women has been strongly held by many ordinary believers over a long period of time.
+ There is a tradition of male domination, going back to the founders of the major religions, that says that it should be followed, as it is a result of divine instruction.
− Many women willingly accept the different role from men that religion requires them to play, seeing the gender hierarchy as a God-given duty for womankind.
− Many religions have 'liberal' strands within them that stress equality between the genders in the eyes of God.

— Women are increasingly making inroads into positions of religious authority; for example, the acceptance of female priests in the Church of England.

Key concepts

patriarchy, monotheism, sexuality, ordination of women

Key thinkers

El Saadawi, McGuire, Barker, Aldridge

Religion and ethnic identity

Key ideas

- 'Identity' has three components: the knowledge that one belongs to a group; the positive or negative values of belonging to a group; and the emotional attachment to a group or distance from other groups.
- Religious identity is therefore the knowledge, values and feelings relating to membership of a religious minority or majority in a society.
- Religion is one of the basic building blocks of ethnic identity, alongside nationality, shared history, language and assumptions about the 'body' (for example genetic inheritance).
- Ethnic identities are multidimensional and also interpenetrative. For example, British Muslims have a shared identity across these dimensions, with a national identity as British citizens, values as members of a British Muslim community and perhaps feelings of belonging to a global Ummah (community of believers).
- Religion provides individuals with many 'markers' of identity, such as customs, dress, food, rituals, celebrations etc., but these are often fluid rather than rigid, e.g. fusion cuisine.
- Religion may also prove a powerful marker of ethnic identity because it can be a means of dealing with 'bafflement', allowing minorities to make sense of their position in society and of discrimination that they may experience.
- In postmodern societies, the fluidity of social relations and the lack of a solid identity in an urban landscape infused with myriad cultures can lead to a turning back to religion as a source of community — the formation of 'neo-tribes'.
- Postmodern uncertainties of identity affect majorities as well as minorities, and Christian as well as non-Christian religious expression.

Evaluation

+ This approach locates religious identity within a set of other sources of identity, but shows the importance of religious belief for marginalised groups in society.
+ It offers a dynamic and open view of identity as not fixed in a traditional formation but as adaptive to the realities of postmodern living.
+ It helps to explain the persistence of religious attachment among certain sections of the population within a generally more secular society.

— Some versions of identity theory fall into 'primordialism', that is, they argue that ethnic communities are 'natural' and exclusivist.

— Identity theory can overemphasise the attachment of young members of ethnic minorities in particular to religious belief, rather than the forms of religious behaviour, as a marker of identity.

— It can assume that ethnic majorities are more secular than ethnic minorities because of their majority position, which means they take their identity for granted.

Key concepts

social identity, Ummah, primordialism, neo-tribes

Key thinkers

Tafjel, Nash, Geertz, Berger, Bauman

Religion and fundamentalism

Key ideas

- Fundamentalism is the strict assertion of the basic beliefs of a religion, often expressed as a belief in the literal truth of the holy book of a religion.
- It can be seen more broadly as a conservative interpretation of faith, in which there is an emphasis on traditional values while the techniques of modernity are accepted as a means of spreading the conservative message.
- Fundamentalism can also be seen as a response by religious individuals and groups to the uncertainties of the postmodern world, with an emphasis on knowing the truth as revealed by their god, and by which they lead their lives.
- While using modern techniques of propaganda, fundamentalism is a profound rejection of modernity and seeks to impose its vision of a holy state on the whole of society.
- It is expressed in different ways in different religions, from the traditional dress of Ultra-Orthodox Jews, who reject the Israeli state, to the jihadis of the Taliban who controlled Afghanistan from 1996 to 2001, the terrorists of al-Qaeda and the New Christian Right political movement in the United States.
- Certain issues become talismanic for fundamentalist beliefs, such as opposition to abortion for some Christians or the wearing of the chador for women under strict Islamic rules.
- What unites all fundamentalists is their dislike of secularism and the liberal consensus of the Western world, which they view as responsible for disorder, crime and sinfulness.
- Education is often a key battleground for fundamentalist groups, whether it concerns the teaching of creationism or intelligent design by the Christian Right or the right of Islamic women to wear the veil under French educational laïcité. The growth of fundamentalist schools is an important political issue.

- Fundamentalists across many religions are united in an anti-homosexual attitude, ranging from opposition to gay marriage in the USA to the public hanging of gay men in Iran.
- In Islam, the growth of fundamentalist belief is associated with the domination of the West over the Muslim world and an anti-Americanism which sees the United States as the 'Great Satan'.

Evaluation

+ The growth of fundamentalist organisations has been prolific and can perhaps be explained as a reaction against postmodernity, in which all metanarratives have been undermined.
+ The events of 11 September 2001 illustrate the challenge of fundamentalism and its claim to be treated as a serious development in religion.
+ Fundamentalism represents an authentic religious response through recalling an era of true religiosity.
− Fundamentalism was born out of the Christian religion and is not easily translated to the other world religions, especially Islam, where the Qur'an is seen as literally the word of God by all Muslims.
− It is uncertain how far fundamentalism has actually grown. As the most vocal of religious groups, fundamentalists tend to dominate religious discourse and drown out the voice of the moderate religious majority.
− Different societies have various responses to the perceived growth of fundamentalism, from political accommodation (the USA under the Republicans) to opposition (Algeria).

Key concepts

literalism, laïcité, talismanic, fundamentalism

Key thinkers

Kepel, Bruce, Modood, Gellner

Secularisation

What is secularisation?

Key ideas

- Many early theorists were hostile to religion and saw its decline as inevitable as reason and science explained what had previously been subject to religious dogma.
- The definition of religion affects whether secularisation can be said to have happened or not. Exclusivist definitions tend to involve secularisation as 'pure' forms of religion evolve to respond to social changes. Inclusivist definitions,

meanwhile, assume that there will always be some form of religion in society as it is essential for the maintenance of good relationships between members.

- The quantum theory of religion suggests that part of human nature is an innate religiosity, which means that religious forms or expressions may change, but religion in one form or another is always with us.
- Secularists believe that there is a logic to history that leads people and societies increasingly to reject religious forms and instead embrace non-religious ideas and behaviours.
- The rationalisation of society, according to Weber, means that people put aside tradition and charisma in favour of reason and science.
- Shiner argues that secularisation has been used by sociologists in at least six different ways, employing as many definitions.
- An overarching definition of secularisation would therefore be 'the loss of influence of religion over society and over individuals'.

Evaluation

+ The definition of secularisation is an important issue because it determines the way that sociologists try to measure it.
+ It is vital to know exactly what is being studied so that sociologists can explore the phenomenon rigorously.
+ Without the concept of secularisation, it would be difficult to examine social change in religious habits and beliefs.
− Definitions can cut off areas of exploration as well as open them up.
− Definitions of secularisation are built up on pre-existing beliefs about the importance of religion. Those who see religion as essential do not accept that secularisation has occurred at all.
− There have been many sociological studies focusing on how to define secularisation rather than exploring the empirical reality of religious behaviour.

Key concepts

secularisation, charisma, rationalisation, science

Key thinkers

Weber, Wilson, Shiner, Robertson, Beckford

Secularisation and society

Key ideas

- The basic notion in looking at society and religion is drawn from Wilson's view that religion 'loses its social significance'.
- This implies that previously well-accepted religious symbols and institutions become less important and lose their status in society.
- This can occur in several ways, such as atrophy or bureaucratisation or the loss of religious thought as a guide to action.

- The process began in Christianity with the Reformation, which introduced choice into religious belief from the unitary world of medieval Catholicism. Choice reduces religion to servicing the needs of distinctive interest groups rather than embodying a whole society.
- The process is called societalisation and is where personal ties are replaced by contractual bonds between individuals, such that the role of the priest as a personal advocate for the individual with God is lost.
- Secular societies welcome social change, while religious societies are resistant. It is therefore the cities, the forges of change, that are the centre of the de-Christianisation of society.
- Religion therefore retreats into the private sphere and loses its public prominence, although vestiges may remain, such as the position of the bishops of the Church of England in the House of Lords.
- This process involves a loss of social status for the clergy and a reduction in the economic power of the church, with a subsequent decline in the proportion of the GDP that is spent on spiritual matters.
- The roles performed by the church are also depleted as societies industrialise and specialised secular agencies emerge to carry out functions originally performed by the church, such as ministering to the poor.
- This loss of functions for the church is accompanied by a shift among the churches to a 'this-worldly' orientation, using advertising techniques to attract adherents and forming unions among small denominations to combat declining attendance.
- Ecumenicalism is therefore a sign of structural weakness rather than a revival of true religious feeling.

Evaluation

+ There has clearly been some decline in the power of the church to influence social policies and historical events in Western societies.
+ Structural differentiation is a feature of modernisation and inevitably involves some loss of functions for religious institutions.
+ The economic and social decline of religious institutions has a physical manifestation in the deconsecration and sale of redundant churches.
− These approaches presuppose a 'golden age of religion', in which there was one dominant religious organisation. Even at the height of Catholic domination of Europe, the church was riven by disputes, heretical movements and subterranean theologies.
− There is a difference between formal attendance at church for social reasons and for the purpose of worship. It may be that there never was any golden age of belief (as opposed to social attendance) from which a decline has occurred.
− The extent to which formal religious institutions have lost power varies from society to society and it may be a Western phenomenon, not paralleled, for example, in Islamic societies.

Key concepts

atrophy, bureaucratisation, societalisation, loss of functions, structural differentiation

Key thinkers

Wilson, Shiner, Berger, Parsons

Religious practices

Key ideas

- At the level of culture, it is argued that there has been a shift of beliefs and behaviour away from a religious or spiritual frame of reference towards a secular frame.
- An example of this shift is the emergence of 'secular' or 'civil' religions, where there are outward signs of religious behaviour but in relation to secular objects. The ideology of Marxism is often cited as an example, with its 'saints', 'icons' and metaphysical belief in a better world.
- These secular beliefs are functional equivalents of religion in a postmodern world and constitute a surrogate religiosity.
- There is also a decline in the observance of religious forms, as measured in a number of ways:
  - There is a drop in the formal membership of the major churches, which is not offset by a rise in those who belong to the more marginal religious groupings.
  - The church is used less frequently for rites of passage such as baptism, marriage and funerals, with the latter still being the most 'popular' use of the church's facilities.
  - There is a fall in the number of people who attend church on either a regular or an occasional basis.
  - Regular Sunday attendance has dropped, as has observance of major festivals such as Christmas, which are more secular than ever before.
  - The growth in alternative forms of entertainment such as television and the internet has led to a fall off in, for example, Sunday school attendance.
- There has been a growth in religious pluralism which has altered the way that individuals practise their beliefs. For example, the growing House Church movement stands outside the traditional churches and is not taken into account in the official statistics for attendance.
- However, the element of choice implicit in religious pluralism suggests a fragmentation of religious behaviour and the potential for individuals to move between religious institutions during their life course.
- Many sects with growing membership are said to be only superficially religious and to function more as religious surrogates, being aimed at secular success rather than representing a return to real religiosity.

Evaluation

+ There is a consistent trend, year on year, towards fewer instances of religious observance, however measured.

+ Rituals and symbols need not have a religious dimension, but may fulfil a human need for pageantry and spectacle rather than a fundamental religiosity.

+ The shift towards secular forms of rites of passage is significant and is reflected in changing legislation, for example that which allows the performance of the marriage ceremony in any licensed location.

− The issue of American exceptionalism is important here. The decline in religious observance has not occurred to the same extent in the United States as it has in Europe. This undermines claims for a general global secularisation.

− There is relatively little decline in the numbers who claim some affiliation to the major religions, and an increase in the numbers who align with sectarian and other forms of religious behaviour.

− There are methodological problems with collecting statistics on attendance and belief that make such statistics suspect and inconclusive.

Key concepts

secular religions, surrogate religiosity, exceptionalism

Key thinkers

Robertson, Bellah, Wilson

Religious consciousness

Key ideas

- Modernity is characterised by a growth in rationality and the disenchantment of the world. This involves individuals discarding myth, charm and poetry to embrace scientific explanations.

- There has been a decline in belief in magic and superstition as natural phenomena become subject to scientific scrutiny.

- The ideology of science has permeated the consciousness of individuals and set up oppositions to irrational beliefs.

- One response of the religious community has been the growth of 'rational' religions that seek to reconcile scientificity with a belief in God. Rational religion is often counterposed to the growth of fundamentalist thinking.

- As the community of believers becomes smaller under the impact of industrialisation, the plausibility structure of religious belief (the institutions and networks that make belief in the irrational possible) is threatened.

- Surveys still show a high proportion of the population who profess a belief in a supernatural being, although the nature of the transcendental being is not always in accordance with traditional religious beliefs.

- As Christianity retreats from the public sphere, the young are much more likely to 'believe without belonging'.

- Knowledge of orthodox religious doctrine is low, as is familiarity with the major text(s) of the religion to which people express an affiliation.

- It is claimed that religious ideas about morality have less of a hold over people's ideas and behaviour as they turn away from religious morality altogether or adopt secular alternatives.
- This is often manifested in the disjunction between the teachings of the church and the behaviour of those who claim strong allegiance to it, for example over birth control.
- Britain could be described as 'post-Christian', with people identifying with some traditional values, such as kindness, but rejecting others, such as sexual Puritanism.

Evaluation

+ The growth in crime and anti-social behaviour is claimed to be the result of the loss of influence of religious morality over individual behaviour.
+ The unpopularity of religious education in schools and the decline in Sunday school attendance result in a lack of exposure to religious ideas among children.
+ Religious festivals, such as Christmas, are increasingly used as secular holidays rather than events imbued with religious meaning.
- Scientific belief-systems cannot provide answers to ultimate questions and thus there will always be a search for the deeper reasons for existence.
- There is still a large reservoir of belief in the subterranean theologies of magic and superstition, as demonstrated by the belief in astrology etc.
- Polling information suggests that the impact of religion on individual consciousness may have diffused, but it still has a strong pull on people's consciences.

Key concepts

disenchantment, plausibility structure, Gods of the Gaps, believing without belonging

Key thinkers

Berger, Wilson, Shiner, Woodhead

Anti-secularisation

Key ideas

- Secularisation theory is accused of being based on a teleological assumption; that is, it is a product of a Marxist/rationalist ideology which holds that, as societies modernise, they will get rid of old-fashioned ideas such as religion.
- Secularisation is therefore built on the back of a simplified view of history as a set of dualisms, in which religious/secular is affixed to traditional/modern.
- Rather than being an objective view of the development of societies, secularism represents an ideology that is unremitting in its hostility to all religious forms.
- Secularisation underestimates the diversity of different patterns of religious behaviour and thought under the conditions of modernity and postmodernity.
- Moreover, it is an ethnocentric view of religious developments, dismissing the persistence of religion in less economically developed countries as a result of their lack of modernity.

- Even in its own terms, secularisation theory does not hold true, as evidenced by the power of religious organisations in contemporary American society and the growth in sects.
- Rather than a decline in religion, society is seeing the growth of a 'new voluntarism' in religion, in which people have choices to make in a self-conscious reflexive process that might result in individuals continuing in the faith of their birth or joining a new form.
- Rational choice theory suggests that humans will always seek out a meaning to life and they make their religious choices by balancing the costs and benefits of adopting a particular belief system.
- In this sense we are religious consumers, calculating the cost of being committed to a particular set of rules and activities and setting this against the promised benefit of redemption.
- Our choices are made on the basis of different forms of religious commitment: the communal (to a community of believers), the ethical (to a belief-system), the cultural (to texts and traditions) and the emotional (to intensity of expression).

Evaluation

+ There is no inevitable decline in religion, rather religious observance varies across time and space and form.
+ The growth of non-standard religious institutions, such as fundamentalist sects, suggests that a religious revival is occurring, negating the secularisation thesis.
+ The development of rational choice theory offers an alternative way of explaining the empirical developments that have taken place.
− The emergence of new religious forms and the need to choose between them can be seen as a fragmentation of religion into a weakened and marginalised set of institutions.
− Secularisation theory is not just concerned with a dualistic view of history, but attempts to explain a complex and multifaceted phenomenon.
− It is difficult to apply the concept of rational individual choice to such an irrational form as religion.

Key concepts

consumerism, rational choice, religious commitment

Key thinkers

Martin, Wilson, Herberg, Bruce, Stark and Bainbridge, Hervieu-Léger, Holden

Questions
&
Answers

In this section, there are four sets of sample questions on the topic of Beliefs in Society. In Samples 1 and 2, questions are followed by specimen student answers, with examiner's comments (indicated by the symbol ). Try to answer these questions first yourself, and then use the example answers and examiner's comments for guidance. Refer back to pages 4 and 5 in the Introduction for advice on the best way to do this.

It is important to note that the way in which the students have answered the questions represents only one appropriate way. You may be able to think of different examples for the shorter questions, and other ways of approaching the longer essay questions.

The questions in Samples 3 and 4 are for you to try without access to student answers and examiner's comments. However, some general guidance is offered on the higher-mark questions in these samples.

Church attendance; religious institutions; young people and belief; functions of religion

1   Read Item A below and answer parts (a) and (b) that follow.

Item A

Church attendance has been in rapid decline in recent decades, with young people less and less likely to be regular church-goers. In studies such as the annual British Social Attitudes Survey, more than half of them say that they regard themselves as not being religious. Yet at the same time, for some young people, religion is a profoundly important part of their lives. So on the one   5
hand, we see growing numbers of young people disengaging from religion, and on the other hand, an increasing intensity of religious devotion among a minority of young people.

Other factors have made this picture of change more complex. For example, since the 1960s, Western societies have seen the emergence of what the sociol-   10
ogist Wade Clark Roof calls an 'expanded spiritual marketplace'. There has been a significant opening up of religious identities, beliefs and activities from the possibilities offered by traditional religious institutions.

Source: adapted from G. Lynch (2007) 'Understanding the sacred', *Sociology Review*, Vol. 17, No. 2.

(a) (i)   Identify and briefly explain *two* reasons why church attendance
has been in rapid decline in recent decades.   (6 marks)
(ii) Identify and briefly explain *one* difference between a church
and a denomination.   (3 marks)
(b) Using material from Item A and elsewhere, assess the reasons why
some young people may show 'an increasing intensity of religious
devotion' (Item A line 7).   (18 marks)

2   Assess the view that religion still performs important functions for
society.   (33 marks)

Total: 60 marks

sample

Answers to Sample 1 questions: grade-A candidate

1 (a) (i) The church as an institution has lost a lot of its power. Once it was a powerful force in society and people felt obliged to attend services, thinking that if they didn't go, they would go to hell. Although still important to some people, the established church generally plays a minor role, and people have either stopped believing or have developed other forms of spirituality which do not require them to go to church.

Another reason is that, until fairly recently, Sundays were still set aside as 'holy days', with no shops open, no sporting fixtures and there was no internet. Nowadays, people have many other things that they can do on Sundays, so prefer to do these things rather than go to church services.

 This is a very full answer; it is possible to score full marks without writing quite so much. Remember that these lower-mark questions do not have to be answered in continuous prose — bullet points are acceptable. The first paragraph contains two reasons: one being that people have stopped believing as the role of the church in society has diminished, the other (and here the candidate has taken a clue from Item A) that some people have developed alternative forms of spirituality. Giving more reasons than are asked for can be a way of trying to ensure that at least two (the required number here) will be correct, but this tactic is not advisable in view of the extra time it takes. The second paragraph gives another acceptable reason, namely the growth of alternative ways of spending time on Sundays. Although this is also linked to the loss of power by the church, it still counts as a further reason.

Overall — two acceptable reasons given, each with some explanation.

6/6 marks

(ii) A church is usually large and wishes to be the dominant religious organisation in society and is often intolerant of other religious beliefs and organisations, while a denomination tends to be smaller and more accepting of other types of belief and religious institutions.

 Again, the candidate offers two differences (size and degree of tolerance), rather than the one asked for, but only 3 marks are available. **3/3 marks**

(b) As Item A points out, although more than half of young people questioned say that they are not religious, some young people see religion as very important in their lives. The 2005 Church Census showed that only about 5% of young people aged 15–19 were regular churchgoers. One thing to point out is that the information in Item A comes from studies such as the British Social Attitudes Survey. It is possible that some young people, who actually do have religious feelings, when questioned said that they were not religious, as they were embarrassed to admit their religiosity, thinking that it was not 'cool'. However, the general trend in British society is for people to be less religious, so we can probably assume that many young people do not have deeply-felt religious beliefs.

🖉 This is a very good opening paragraph. It refers directly to Item A, as asked by the question, and does more than simply paraphrase or quote directly. Good knowledge and understanding are shown by giving an example which supports the information in Item A, thus fulfilling the 'and elsewhere' part of the question. The candidate also uses Item A to point out a possible flaw in the survey method, namely, that people may not always give truthful answers. Having pointed out a possible flaw, the candidate then shows evaluation by linking the statement about the loss of religiosity among young people to a more general trend in society.

Though not much research has been carried out into young people and religious belief, in 2005 David Voas published some research on this issue. He found that, where there were two religious parents in a family, they had a 50:50 chance of passing on their religious beliefs to their children. Where there was only one religious parent, there was only a one-in-four chance of the children being religious, while where neither parent was religious, the children were also likely to have no religious belief. This suggests that those young people who are religious probably come from 'religious' families. Again, as the number of religious adults declines, it is likely that there will be fewer religious young people, unless they become religious converts when they are older.

🖉 This paragraph continues to focus on the question of children/young people and religious devotion, quoting some relevant research and then going on to show good knowledge, understanding and analysis.

There is, however, another reason why some young people may show 'an increasing intensity of religious devotion', and it highlights the problems of thinking only about Christianity. For many young people from ethnic minority families, living in Britain is not easy, and they may feel marginalised and excluded from mainstream society. For many of these young people, religion becomes an important part of their identity, and provides them with a sense of community and belonging. This seems to be the case with many young Muslims. Research by Mirza et al. (2007) showed that religious identity and values were increasingly important to second and third generation young Muslims. Whereas their parents tended to try to 'blend in' and adapt to the British way of life, younger Muslims are increasingly prepared to express their religious identity publicly. For example, many young Muslim girls and women choose to wear the hijab, even though their mothers do not do so. Mirza et al. also argue that many of the measures designed to protect Muslims and acknowledge their different religious beliefs, such as anti-racist laws, faith schools etc. serve to reinforce the idea that Muslims are 'different', and can emphasise the importance of a separate religious identity.

Other young people in groups at risk of being marginalised, such as Afro-Caribbeans, may also show increasing religious devotion, especially where they are brought up in Pentecostal or other evangelical Christian families. Again, as with the early sects, religious belief and membership of a religious

community can act as a buffer and compensate for social exclusion, poverty and deprivation.

These two paragraphs remain tightly focused on the set question, and show a sound knowledge and understanding of the issues. There is good and accurate knowledge of relevant research, and reference is made to two different religious faiths, with a nice link made between current evangelical Christianity and early Christian sects.

In conclusion, there are a number of reasons why some young people may show increased religious devotion. While in some cases it is because of family upbringing, in others it reflects social exclusion and the decline of other forms of social identity, such as work, neighbourhood and social class.

The candidate attempts here to draw the arguments together to form a conclusion. This kind of conclusion, which is in effect a brief summary of the arguments and evidence presented in the main part of the answer, can be very effective, as is the case here. Remember that, with an 18-mark question such as this, only 20–25 minutes should be spent on the answer, so it is not expected that candidates will be able to present all the arguments and evidence at their disposal. This candidate has done as much as can be reasonably expected in the time available and has stuck closely to the set question.

AO1: 6/6 + AO2: 11/12 = **17/18 marks**

2   The view that social institutions continue to exist because they perform important functions for society is, of course, a functionalist view. Durkheim, a major functionalist and one of the founding fathers of sociology, believed that one of religion's main functions was to bring the people of a society together, and to reinforce social norms and values. However, much of Durkheim's ideas about this were formed from the study of simple, small-scale societies or even tribes, so it is arguable whether this view can be applied to large-scale societies, particularly modern or postmodern ones, with their complex structure and multitude of different religious faiths. Bellah, a neo-functionalist, also believes that religion still performs essential functions. He says that a process of individuation has occurred, leaving people to look for religious meaning through individual experience, rather than through an organisation such as an established church.

A good opening paragraph, which immediately locates the view expressed in the question to a particular social theory and a sociologist. Having briefly explained what Durkheim regarded as one of religion's major functions, the candidate shows evaluation by pointing out a possible problem with the view. Good knowledge and understanding is also shown by referring to the views of a neo-functionalist.

Another classical sociologist, Karl Marx, thought that religious beliefs were based on superstition, and that the traditional forms of religion would disappear once rational, scientific knowledge became more widespread in society. Marx believed that religion served to bring comfort to the oppressed working class, and it could be argued that enforced changes in the way that capitalists treated their workers, together with the development of the welfare state, would lessen the need for religious beliefs as a source of comfort.

🖉 The candidate here shows further knowledge and understanding of sociological theory, presenting a contrasting view to that of Durkheim. Note that the candidate has yet to address the set question directly. This is still fine at this point, but remember that it is important to keep an eye on the time, and to make sure that you do not spend too long before getting down to the 'meat' of your answer.

It is obvious, not only from Britain but from many other countries that, even though there is evidence of growing secularisation, religion is still important to many people on a personal level, and that religious institutions still have some power. Is this linked to the functions it performs, and if it is, what are those functions?

Despite the changes in society and a possible move towards more meritocracy, it is true that some people are still marginalised and oppressed. For them, religious beliefs can bring hope of a better life in the next world, and comfort and support to help with the pain of this world. It could be argued that having this comfort prevents such people from becoming more radical and demanding change. For those in power, this could be seen as an important function for society, as it serves to prevent radical change and possible social upheaval.

🖉 The candidate now moves to addressing the set question directly, and gives one example of a possibly important function performed by religion. It would be helpful to give an example of a marginalised or oppressed group for whom religion could provide comfort. Note that analysis and evaluation are shown by suggesting that only some people ('those in power') might see the possible prevention of radicalisation as functionally important.

In some countries, such as Britain, there is a divide between religious institutions and the state, although the Church of England has a role to play in certain state functions (the coronation of the monarch) and some of its bishops sit in the House of Lords. Some people argue, though, that religious organisations such as the Church of England are important because they can provide a check to the power of the state. Leading church leaders, such as the Archbishop of Canterbury, have spoken out against social issues such as poverty, and some of those who take part in protests — for example against the war in Iraq — have strong religious views. Again, the British state has made some concessions to religious beliefs, for example, allowing animals to be slaughtered according to Jewish and Islamic laws.

In the USA, religious leaders such as Martin Luther King were important figures in the Civil Rights movement, and the efforts of these leaders and their followers helped to force the American state to end segregation and discrimination against black Americans.

🖉 An interesting couple of paragraphs, looking at how religion can sometimes act as a buffer against the power of the state and provide a means of social protest. Note

that the candidate provides a relevant example from another society, which shows breadth of knowledge.

Another important function of religion in modern Britain (as it was in the past) is to provide various welfare functions, often seen today as 'plugging the gaps' in the welfare state. For example, the Salvation Army provides funds and shelter for individuals and families in need, and also runs a service giving information about runaway children to let their family know that they are alright. Other religious organisations provide help and support for drug and alcohol addicts and people with AIDS and even run adoption agencies. Many religious groups also raise money for aid to poor countries.

✐ The candidate provides further relevant examples of some important functions performed by religious groups.

However, there are also arguments that religion is sometimes dysfunctional for society, or at least some parts of it. The 'right to life' movement, in the UK but especially in the USA, has caused not just distress but also actual harm to women seeking an abortion and doctors involved in providing abortions. The teachings of the Roman Catholic Church against contraception and divorce can also be seen as dysfunctional for some families, even though many followers do not obey the Pope, especially where contraception is concerned. The radicalisation of some young Muslims, leading to terror attacks in Britain and the USA, is another example of where religion can be dysfunctional. Again, the Taliban in Afghanistan have proved very dysfunctional to females, stopping girls from going to school and not letting women work outside the home or have similar freedoms to men. It can, therefore, be argued that not all the roles played by religion in society are good.

✐ Evaluation is shown here by offering some well chosen examples of where religion can be seen as dysfunctional. Note that the candidate recognises that certain groups may be more affected than others by these aspects of religion.

In conclusion, it can be seen that, even in so-called secular societies, religion can perform important functions. However, some aspects of religion can also be dysfunctional, both for groups of individuals and for society.

✐ A brief but adequate conclusion reminding the examiner that the candidate has discussed both positive and negative aspects of the functions performed by religion and religious organisations.

AO1: 13/15 + AO2 (a): 7/9 + AO2 (b): 9/9 = **29/33 marks**

Overall: 55/60 marks

Answers to Sample 1 questions: grade-C candidate

1 **(a) (i)** ● Lots of people believe in things such as New Age spiritualism, which means that they have faith but don't go to church.
          ● Society has become more secular.

🖉 The candidate is correct in thinking that in these very short questions giving bullet-point answers is acceptable. The first point identifies a reason (belief in New Age spiritualism) and gives a brief explanation of how this is linked to (non) church attendance. This is just enough to score 3 marks. However, the second point gives a reason, but with no explanation, so gains only 1 mark. **4/6 marks**

(ii) Churches are usually more formal than denominations.

🖉 The candidate gives an acceptable difference, but there is no attempt to offer an explanation of what 'more formal' means in this context, so this answer gains only 1 mark. **1/3 marks**

(b) As Item A says, there is an increasing intensity of religious devotion among a minority of young people. In some cases this could be due to peer pressure, such as the 'Silver Ring Thing' among some American girls, where they wear a ring as a promise not to have sex before they are married.

🖉 Although the candidate makes an immediate reference to Item A, it is just to repeat a phrase; there is no discussion or development. While reference to Item A is important, the material should be used in some way to present or develop an argument. At this point, it looks as though the candidate has already moved on, though further appropriate reference may be made later. A potentially relevant example is offered, but the candidate does not draw out how wearing the silver ring is linked to religious devotion. The examiners are all sociologists, but even so, you should try to make sure that they can see that you understand the significance of what you are writing in terms of the set question.

As Britain is now a mainly secular society, with religion losing social significance, it seems strange that some young people are becoming more religious. However, it is mainly the established Christian churches that are declining, and many young people will have been brought up in other faiths, e.g. Islam or Sikhism. These are usually more religious than Christianity, so some of the young people could come from these backgrounds.

🖉 There is some evidence that the candidate understands what is meant by 'secular', and a good point is made about the decline in established Christian churches rather than across all faiths and types of religious organisation. However, it is not clear exactly what is meant by the statement that faiths such as Islam or Sikhism are 'more religious' than Christianity. Again, the candidate is not spelling out clearly the line of argument. Even answers to shorter essay questions should show a clear line of argument, with supporting points and evidence.

Some immigrants to Britain, even from Christian countries such as Poland, are more religious than native British people, and many of these immigrants are younger, so this could also be an explanation of why some young people are religious. Some people from ethnic minority groups might want to express their solidarity with Muslims from other countries as a result of the 'war on terror'

and the war in Iraq. This could mean that they felt stronger links to their religion and it became more important to them.

☑ Some good points here.

Item A doesn't say what people meant by 'religious', so some answers could have been referring to non-traditional religious beliefs and practices such as New Ageism or spiritualism.

☑ Another reference to Item A, and an evaluative point referring to the lack of information about whether or not there was a shared definition of 'religious' in the studies/surveys, which is potentially an important issue. However, the point about non-traditional beliefs and practices should be developed — why might young people be attracted to such beliefs? The answer ends very abruptly, without any attempt at a conclusion. There are several missed opportunities here, resulting in lost marks for this candidate.   AO1: 3/6 + AO2: 8/12 = **11/18 marks**

2   Although Britain is now considered to be a secular society, religion still seems to be important. Though church attendance is falling, some people still attend church regularly, and some churches are even growing. In surveys about religious belief, most people say that they have some kind of belief or faith, though sometimes this is in a 'spirit' or 'life force' rather than God.

☑ The knowledge presented here is accurate and potentially relevant to the question. However, the candidate has not yet picked up on the idea of the 'functions' of religion, and whether or not these are important. It is usually a good idea to make a clear reference to the set question (without simply repeating it) as soon as possible in your answer. This can help to keep you on the right track.

Many sociologists thought that, as scientific ideas became more widespread, the need for religious explanations of the world would disappear, or at least decrease, but this doesn't really seem to be the case. Richard Dawkins is attacked by many people for his views on religion and his atheistic beliefs, and even David Attenborough has said that he receives hate mail from people because he doesn't acknowledge or praise God in his programmes about the wonders of wildlife. The argument about teaching creationism in schools highlights the fact that some people still prefer religious beliefs to scientific ones.

☑ The candidate now seems in danger of ignoring the issues raised by the question, and seems to be offering an answer on secularisation. It is really important to make sure that your answer addresses the set question, and this is where a brief essay plan can help. Note that the information here is largely general, without a clear sociological focus.

Again, while the power of the church is much less than it was in medieval times, it still has power. Church of England bishops sit in the House of Lords, and Roman Catholics the world over accept the power of the Pope to tell them how they should live their lives. If we look at other religions, Islam in particular is a powerful force in society, and has shown (e.g. in Iran) how religious ideas can bring about social change, such as the overthrow of the shah. Marxists argue that, under some circumstances, religion can bring about social change rather than always supporting the status quo.

📝 There is still no focus on the set question, and the candidate is likely to lose many valuable marks by not using arguments and evidence clearly relevant to the question asked. Can you think of ways in which at least some of the information presented could be made relevant to the set question? There is a reference to social theory in the last sentence, but this, too, is not linked to the question.

So why is religion still important for society? For some people it brings comfort — for example, people who are poor or oppressed. For some immigrants it reminds them of home, such as the many Polish people who are practising Roman Catholics. Some Muslims see their religious beliefs as an important part of their identity, as their religion covers all aspects of their lives. Functionalists argue that social institutions only last if they are important for society, although some can become dysfunctional over time.

📝 The candidate at last begins to focus on the reasons for the importance of religion, although the reference to 'functions' is still implicit. The examples presented focus on the importance to individuals, rather than to society. This is legitimate, although some link should be provided regarding why importance to individuals might also be important to society. The last sentence is, of course, relevant, and in a good answer would be developed further. Here it appears to be added almost as a last-minute afterthought.

Again, religion can act to bring people together. There are often religious ceremonies and services after disasters or personal tragedies, such as the remembrance service for Princess Diana, and the church services after the 11 September bombings in the USA, the tsunami and the Australian bush fires. It is thought that taking part in acts of collective worship helps people to cope with their grief, and also acts as a mark of respect. It could also help people to think of the disaster as an act of God, rather than the fault of a person, company or government.

📝 Here there is an attempt to look at the possible functions of religion for society. The line of argument is still presented largely through examples. While examples are a good way of showing appropriate knowledge and understanding, they should always be linked to clear sociological arguments.

Finally, it is getting more and more difficult to talk about religion. As well as the major world religions, there has been a growth in 'pick'n'mix' religion, with people turning to various types of New Age beliefs, and some people joining cults and sects. For some people, this kind of belief can help them to express themselves as individuals, or find support and comfort being in a group of people with shared beliefs. So, although Britain is in one sense mainly a secular society, religion still performs important functions.

This paragraph raises a potentially very important point, namely what exactly do we mean by religion? If you can raise this issue earlier, it will give you the opportunity to engage in a sociological debate, while still focusing on the issue of 'functions'. Overall, this is a weak conclusion. The candidate has missed the opportunity to present the sociological arguments and so has been unable to present a stronger and more relevant conclusion.

AO1: 8/15 + AO2 (a): 5/9 + AO2 (b): 3/9 = **16/33 marks**

Overall: 32/60 marks

Sample 2

Defining religion; sects; religion and social change

1   Read Item A below and answer parts (a) and (b) that follow.

Item A

There have been many attempts to arrive at a clear definition of a sect. Weber's ideal type defined the sect largely in terms of how it differed from a church. For example, membership of a sect is usually by conversion, whereas many people are born into a particular church, and do not have to prove anything to become a member. Some sects arise when a group breaks away from an established religious organisation, often as a result of a disagreement over doctrine. Wallis defined a sect in terms of its relationship to the world, i.e. whether it was 'world-affirming' or 'world-rejecting'. Many sects emphasise their exclusiveness — only those who show themselves to be worthy are accepted as members. It is suggested that membership of sects increases in times of rapid social change, when both personal anxiety and social disorganisa-tion may be high. It is important to remember that sects can arise from religions other than Christianity, for example the Falun Gong of China and the Aum Shinrikyo of Japan.

   (a) (i)   Identify and briefly explain *two* problems of defining what is
            meant by 'religion'.   (6 marks)
      (ii) Identify and briefly explain *one* reason why some sects are
            short-lived.   (3 marks)
   (b) Using material from Item A and elsewhere, assess the problems
       of measuring the extent of sect membership in society.   (18 marks)
2   'Far from always being a conservative force in society, religious beliefs
     can act to promote social change.' To what extent is this view supported
     by sociological arguments and evidence?   (33 marks)

Total: 60 marks

■ ■ ■

Answers to Sample 2 questions: grade-A candidate

1   (a) (i)   Some sociologists use an 'inclusivist' definition, which accepts belief
              systems without reference to a god or supernatural being, while others use
              'exclusivist' definitions, which say that there has to be some reference to
              a supernatural being or beings with powers to affect life on earth.

              We need to know what counts as 'religious'. Do we mean people who just
              say that they have a religious belief, or only people who show some kind
              of religious commitment, e.g. praying or going to services?

2

sample

e Two good reasons, each with a clear explanation. **6/6 marks**

(ii) The sect only exists because of a charismatic leader.

e This is an acceptable reason, but there is no attempt to offer an explanation of why this might make the sect short-lived — for example when the leader dies and there is no replacement. Remember that it is necessary to give a suitable reason, plus a brief explanation to gain full marks. **1/3 marks**

(b) As Item A suggests, there are different ways of defining exactly what a sect is. Sometimes, particularly in the mass media, the terms 'sect' and 'cult' are used as if they were the same thing, though there are differences between them, one being that the cult is usually less structured and organised than the sect. If sociologists do not have a shared definition of what we mean by a sect, there is an obvious problem in defining how many people are sect members.

e A good start — it makes immediate and relevant reference to Item A and goes on to identify an important difficulty of measuring the extent of sect membership.

Sometimes a sect arises as a breakaway movement from a church, often because some people disagree with the teachings or leadership. Examples of this would be the Baptists and Congregationalists. However, we now regard these groups as denominations, so another problem is the point in time at which the sect is measured. If one difference between a sect and a denomination is the level of organisation, how much organisation does there have to be before we decide that something is a denomination and not a sect?

e A good paragraph. Note how the candidate first gives a way in which a sect might arise, then gives some examples of where this has happened, and then links this to the problem outlined in the question.

Another problem is that, as Item A points out, some sects are 'world-rejecting' (Wallis). This means that they avoid contact with the wider society, and are often very secretive. It would be difficult in these cases for a sociologist to find out how many people were members, as members of these sects tend to live in closed communities. Eileen Barker is one of the few sociologists to do in-depth research into a sect, with her work *The Making of a Moonie*.

e Another relevant reference to Item A — which is then explained — linked to the problem raised by the question and finished off with an appropriate example.

If a sect is world-affirming, it still could be difficult to measure the extent of membership as some of these sects (e.g. the TM movement) are very secretive and have a 'shifting' membership, in that people seem to move in and out, so it would depend on the point at which membership was measured.

e Another appropriate difficulty identified and explained. This candidate clearly understands the methodological problem of the importance of the particular point in time at which something is measured.

It is hard to see how sociologists could easily measure sect membership just by asking people about their religious beliefs and practices. Apart from the sheer size of such a survey (sect membership is quite low, so you would have to ask a lot of people to find some sect members), many people would not give you that information anyway, especially if the sect was one that was engaged in activities that were criminal (e.g. the Japanese Supreme Truth) or suicidal (e.g. Heaven's Gate). This means that, in some cases, the only way would be for a participant observation study, which, with some sects, would have to be covert. This would be very time-consuming, and could be dangerous, if the sect was engaged in criminal activities.

🖉 A further example of the problems of measuring sect membership, supported by some appropriate examples and also showing knowledge of methodological issues.

In conclusion, it is very difficult to measure the extent of sect membership in society.

🖉 This is a weak conclusion, which neither summarises the discussion nor adds anything to it. However, overall this is a good answer, showing the need for a tight focus in this type of 18-mark question.   AO1: 6/6 + AO2: 10/12 = **16/18 marks**

2 The idea that religion acts as a conservative force in society is associated with the functionalists. Durkeim believed that, through shared rituals and beliefs, religion created social solidarity, and the passing on of these beliefs and rituals helped to maintain the status quo. However, Marx also saw religion mainly as a conservative force, as he believed that it had an ideological role, namely supporting capitalism and helping to maintain the power of the capitalists.

🖉 This is a good opening paragraph, clearly linked to the question and showing good knowledge and understanding by accurate reference to the views of two classical sociologists.

The idea that religion can promote social change is usually associated with Max Weber. In his 'Protestant ethic' thesis, Weber tried to show that, under certain conditions, religious beliefs could make people act in such a way that social change took place. Weber's example was of the Calvinists, whose beliefs led them to work hard in their 'calling' but not to spend their money on worldly goods and luxuries. In this way, they amassed a great deal of capital which they could invest in the new technologies and working practices that underpinned the Industrial Revolution.

🖉 The candidate now moves on to discuss the ideas of religion and social change, again using a classical sociologist to show good knowledge and understanding of social theory. Note how the temptation to give a lengthy description of Weber's work has been avoided. With limited time at your disposal, it is a good idea to be as brief as possible while still getting the ideas across. In this way, you can show greater breadth.

However, Gramsci — a neo-Marxist — showed how the ideas of religion could be interpreted in a way that was different from what the capitalists intended; for example, believing that religion said that it was a duty to help the poor and oppressed. This leads to the idea of liberation theology, a movement in 1960s and 1970s Latin America, in which religious leaders — mainly Catholic priests — helped to fight poverty and injustice in the name of religion. Gramsci said that no group could achieve total hegemony, so there was always some room for different interpretations.

This is evaluation of the classical Marxist idea by juxtaposition, meaning that the candidate has used another perspective to show how Marxist ideas can be used in a different way.

The views of religious fundamentalists, such as the New Christian Right in America, can also be used to bring about social change. The NCR forms a strong political force and has successfully managed in some states to bring about changes in the law — for example with regard to abortion and gay marriage — where it has managed to overturn or prevent more liberal policies on these issues. It is still fighting these and other matters, such as the teaching of creationism rather than evolution in schools.

Though brief, this paragraph provides interesting examples of the influence of certain religious ideas.

If we look at other religions, not just at Christianity, we can also see that sometimes religious ideas are linked to social change. A good example would be the revolution in Iran, in which the shah was overthrown and the ayatollahs, or religious leaders, took control. There are other examples of religious fundamentalism where people's beliefs and practices have brought about social change. We could think of the many ways that Western society has changed, with the so-called 'war on terror' following the 11 September attacks in the USA and the 7 July attacks in London. Again, the very strict interpretation of Islamic law by the Taliban in Afghanistan has led to changes in that society, many of them with negative effects on women and girls, who have far less freedom than they did before.

This is a very good paragraph, showing wide-ranging knowledge and understanding of religious ideas other than Christian ones that are linked to social change.

In conclusion, while many religious ideas and practices have been, and still are, linked to maintaining the status quo, there are many examples in society where they are also linked to bringing about social change.

This is a brief but adequate conclusion, in which the candidate reminds the reader of the preceding arguments and evidence.

AO1: 12/15 + AO2 (a): 8/9 + AO2 (b): 8/9 = **28/33 marks**

Overall: 51/60 marks

Answers to Sample 2 questions: grade-C candidate

1 **(a) (i)** Deciding whether there has to be a belief in a god or being with supernatural powers, or just a belief in some kind of 'life force' with no special power to influence worldly affairs.

How you define religion affects the results.

e The first point made is an acceptable problem, with an adequate explanation. However, the second point is not clear (what results?) and is rather a consequence of the problems of definition, rather than a problem of definition in its own right. So, 3/3 for the first point, 0/3 for the second. **3/6 marks**

(ii) Some 'world-rejecting' sects could be so strict and make life so hard for their members that people won't stay and will leave the group.

e This is an acceptable reason with a suitable explanation. **3/3 marks**

(b) As Item A says, there have been many attempts to arrive at a clear definition of a sect. Some sects have made headlines around the world — for example the members of the Branch Davidians at Waco and the mass suicide of the members of the People's Temple at Jonestown and the Heaven's Gate members. People might not have even heard of these sects if people hadn't died because of them.

e This candidate has clearly been instructed about the importance of making reference to Item A. However, all that happens here is that the first sentence is reproduced and then the candidate goes on to talk about something entirely different. To gain higher marks, the candidate would need to make the point that attempts to measure sect membership will be affected by the definition (of a sect) that is used. There are, however, three examples of sects given and the implicit suggestion that there has to be knowledge of the existence of a sect before there can be any attempt to gauge its membership.

It is easier to measure sect membership if the sect is world affirming, because there won't be a need for secrecy — the sect might even advertise for members, or publish membership lists. A lot of world rejecting sects are very secretive, and cut themselves off from the world, so it would be hard for a sociologist to know about these, except through covert participant observation, which could be difficult and dangerous.

e The use of the terms 'world affirming' and 'world rejecting' is implicit reference to Item A, and the candidate gives acceptable reasons why it might be easier to measure membership of the first scenario than the second. No reasons are given regarding why covert participant observation might be 'difficult and dangerous', though there is clearly understanding of the method and the circumstances under which it might be used. Remember that it is important, where relevant, to make reference to sociological theories and methods.

sample

Item A says that membership of sects increases in times of rapid social change. This could be another problem of measurement. If there is a lot of social change, then people could join a sect but just for a short while, and then move out or move away or join a different one. So you could get different numbers depending on when you did the counting.

Here the candidate's reference to Item A is followed by a clear link to the question.

Another problem of measurement could be when looking at sects in other societies, such as the ones mentioned in Item A. There would be difficulties for Western sociologists to get knowledge of these sects unless they spoke the language, and also the sect could be engaged in illegal activities, like the gas attack on the Japanese underground.

Further difficulties of measuring sect membership are given, again using Item A, and knowledge is shown of the activities of the Aum Shinrikyo sect, though the reference is not made explicit. There are other problems of measurement, which are not mentioned here, but in a shorter-mark question it is not usually necessary or possible to include all points. The candidate shows reasonable knowledge and understanding here, though analysis and evaluation are relatively weak.

Last, as Item A says, there is no clear definition of what we mean by a sect. Different sociologists could have different ideas, which would affect the outcome. It also takes a long time to do research, so by the time it was finished, it could already be out of date.

The candidate finally picks up on this important point raised by Item A, and also offers a further problem of measuring the extent of sect membership. There is no attempt to write a conclusion. AO1: 4/6 + AO2: 7/12 = **11/18 marks**

2 Marx said that religion was ideological, that it made the workers believe that everything was according to God's plan, so that it justified the power of the capitalists. Religious ideas served two purposes, to keep the existing social order and to give the oppressed working class comfort, as they were promised that life would be better in the next world.

The candidate has jumped straight in here. Marxist ideas on religion are presented, though the link to these and religion being a conservative force in society is largely implicit.

Weber said that religion caused social change. He believed that the ideas of the Protestant work ethic brought about capitalism and the Industrial Revolution, which was a huge social change. Countries without the Protestant work ethic took much longer to industrialise.

The summary of Weber's thesis is not quite accurate, but the notion of the link between the Protestant work ethic and social change is evident.

Religion can also be a conservative force when it won't allow for new ideas. This happened when Galileo tried to show that the earth moved round the sun, and not the other way round, which was the teaching of the church. He was tried for heresy and spent the last years of his life under house arrest. Religious conservatism is also shown in the fact that the Christian religion did not want to accept women priests (Roman Catholics still don't) or allow divorced couples to marry in church.

> 🖉 Further examples of religion acting as a conservative force. However, the main thrust of the question concerns religion and social change, so the candidate needs to begin to address this aspect of the question in more detail.

Liberation theology shows that religion can promote social change. Priests in South America worked hard to improve the lot of the oppressed workers, saying that Jesus taught that you should help the poor in society. Fundamentalists also want social change. In their case, they want to 'turn back the clock' and return to what they consider to be the original beliefs and practices of their religion. To do this, they want to get rid of what they see as the immoral practices seen in modern society and 'get back to basics'. In some cases they have succeeded, e.g. the Iranian revolution.

The new US president, Barack Obama, is a religious man who believes that it is his duty to improve the condition of the black US population, who were among his strongest supporters. However, George W. Bush was also religious (a born-again Christian) and he was right-wing and did little to help the poor of the USA, so we see that religion can be a conservative force and a force for social change.

> 🖉 Some relevant examples of religious ideas linked to social change, and an interesting example of the religious beliefs of the two latest US presidents. There is no conclusion as such, though the last part of the final sentence attempts to bring the two parts of the question together.

Functionalists like Durkheim also believe that religion is conservative. He believed that when people worshipped their god (or totem pole), they were in fact worshipping their own society. Durkheim said that coming together in acts of worship reminded people of what were the shared norms and values of their society. This made it harder for people to go against those norms, and so helped to keep the society stable and unchanging. Durkheim has been criticised, though, for looking at very small simple societies, and some sociologists say that his ideas aren't relevant to today's society.

> 🖉 It looks very much as though this paragraph is an afterthought, and shows the need for even a brief plan before starting on an essay. Nevertheless, the material is broadly accurate and relevant to the question, in that it presents another sociological view on religion acting as a conservative force in society.
>
> AO1: 9/15 + AO2 (a): 6/9 + AO2 (b): 5/9 = **20/33 marks**
>
> **Overall: 37/60 marks**

Sample 3

Religious observance; church attendance and age; church attendance and ethnicity; religious fundamentalism

1 Read Item A below and answer parts (a) and (b) that follow.

Item A

The major findings from the 2005 Church Census, undertaken by Christian Research, show that many churches in England are in a healthier state now than 7 years ago. Some local churches, as well as a few denominations, are doing very well, more churches are growing, and overall they are not losing nearly as many people as they were. The Census showed that in the 1990s, 1 million people left church in 9 years, but in the 7 years from 1998 to 2005, only half a million left, a much slower rate of decline. There are two major reasons for this slowing decline: the number of churches which are growing, and a considerable increase of ethnic minority churchgoers, especially black people. However, the declining churches are still losing more people than the growing churches are gaining. The net effect is that overall, 6.3% of the population are now in church on an average Sunday, down from 7.5% in 1998. A major factor in this decline is that churchgoers are significantly older on average than the population — 29% of churchgoers are 65 or over, compared with 16% of the population.

Source: adapted from P. Brierley (2006) *Pulling out of the Nosedive*, Christian Research.

    (a) (i) Identify and briefly explain *two* possible problems with the way in which attendance at religious services is measured. (6 marks)

    (ii) Identify and briefly explain *one* reason why older people may attend church more frequently than younger people. (3 marks)

    (b) Using material from Item A and elsewhere, assess some of the reasons for the increase in churchgoers from ethnic minority backgrounds. (18 marks)

2 Assess the view that the rise of religious fundamentalism poses a threat to the stability of society. (33 marks)

Total: 60 marks

■ ■ ■

Guidance

Question 1 (b)

Remember to use Item A. There are two aspects that would help you. The first is the reference to some 'local churches' that are growing — remember that immigrants, especially recent ones, tend to cluster in certain geographical areas. The second point refers to 'black people' — why might such people be more likely to attend church? Think of some of the ways in which religious attendance and membership of a church might have a particular appeal for some black people. Think of the characteristics of class, age and identity.

Question 2

Here you would need to show that you understand what is meant by 'religious fundamentalism', and then explain why it might be thought to pose a threat to the stability of society. Remember that you do not have to focus only on aspects of 'terror' — there are other circumstances in which religious fundamentalists might wish to change their society. Remember also that many religious fundamentalists are conservative, and that religious fundamentalism is found in all major religions. This is a question that allows you to make good use of relevant examples.

ample 4

Religion and patriarchy; sect membership; alternative forms of spirituality; secularisation, religion and science

1 Read Item A below and answer parts (a) and (b) that follow.

Item A

There is little or no consensus regarding what is happening to the sacred in contemporary Britain. Some, for example, state that the sacred is simply disappearing. The *secularisation* theorists point to evidence of decline, in particular to the apparently relentless decline of church attendance in Britain. Others, however, claim that New Age spiritualities are a growing force. *Sacralisation* theorists point to evidence of growth, in particular to the ever-increasing popularity of New Age practices.

The 'spiritual revolution thesis' is thus comprised of two, empirically testable, components. The first is that the sacred is most likely to be in decline when it operates by way of overarching authority structures which tell people how they *ought* to live their lives. The second is that the sacred is more likely to be growing when it takes the form of an inner spirituality which has to do with discovering 'the real or whole me'.

Source: adapted from P. Heelas and L. Woodhead (2003) 'The Kendal Project', *Sociology Review*, Vol. 13, No. 2.

(a) (i) **Identify and briefly explain *one* way in which religion may be seen as being patriarchal.** (3 marks)

(ii) **Identify and briefly explain *two* reasons why membership of a sect might appeal to some people from underprivileged groups.** (6 marks)

(b) **Using material from Item A and elsewhere, assess some of the reasons for the apparent growth in alternative forms of spirituality.** (18 marks)

2 **'We now live in a secular society in which religious explanations of the natural world have been replaced by scientific ones.' To what extent do sociological arguments and evidence support this view of modern Britain?** (33 marks)

Total: 60 marks

■ ■ ■

Guidance

Question 1 (b)

Item A tells you that it is sacralisation theorists who argue that New Age practices are a growing force. You need to show that you understand what is meant by 'New Age' practices, and what the link is to the so-called secularisation thesis. You also need to be able to show what it is about these practices that allow sacralisation theorists to claim that they are 'spiritual', and how this view is contested by other sociologists. Note that the question refers to the 'apparent growth' in alternative forms of spirituality, suggesting that this is a contested view. If you are able to do so, you would find it helpful to look up the original article (see the source details below Item A) and also the article by Voas and Bruce, which is a critique of this view (*Sociology Review*, Vol. 15, No. 4, April 2006).

Question 2

Make sure that you note that this is not a simple question about secularisation. It really is important here to focus on the actual question set, which is the extent to which religious explanations of the natural world have been replaced by scientific ones. Note that the question refers to 'sociological arguments and evidence'. This means that you must show knowledge of relevant sociological theories, as well offering relevant examples. Therefore, you need to show which sociologists are associated with the view that religious explanations would be replaced by scientific ones, and state briefly what their arguments are. Then you need to be able to give examples of cases (note that the question refers to 'modern Britain') in which their arguments seem to be upheld (i.e. the acceptance of scientific explanations) and where such arguments seem to be refuted. In the second scenario, you might discuss the issue of the teaching of creationism, and also give examples of groups that have a belief in the literal truth of the Bible — or other holy book, if your discussion goes beyond Christianity. You might usefully address the question of whether the acceptance of scientific explanations rather than religious ones inevitably means that a society is secular. Finally, on the basis of the evidence presented, you will need to offer a conclusion regarding the extent to which the statement in the question appears to be supported.